Scrumptious
Toppers
for Tots and Toddlers

Scrumptious Toppers

for Tots and Toddlers

30 HATS AND CAPS FROM

Debby Ware

The Taunton Press

Text © 2008 by Debby Ware
Photographs © 2008 by James Roderick
Illustrations © 2008 by The Taunton Press, Inc.

The Taunton Press
Inspiration for hands-on living®

The Taunton Press, Inc., 63 South Main Street,
PO Box 5506, Newtown, CT 06470-5506

e-mail: tp@taunton.com

EDITORS: Erica Sanders-Foege, Courtney Jordan
COPY EDITOR: Betty Christiansen
JACKET/COVER DESIGN: Teresa Fernandez
INTERIOR DESIGN & LAYOUT: Deborah Kerner
ILLUSTRATOR: Christine Erikson
PHOTOGRAPHER: James Roderick

The following manufacturers/names appearing in *Scrumptious Toppers for Tots and Toddlers* are trademarks: Lion Brand Yarns Chenille Quick & Thick®, Lion Brand Yarns Homespun®, Velcro®

Library of Congress Cataloging-in-Publication Data
Ware, Debby, 1952-
  Scrumptious toppers for tots and toddlers : 30 hats and caps from Debby Ware / Debby Ware.
     p. cm.
  Includes bibliographical references and index.
  ISBN 978-1-56158-998-2 (alk. paper)
  1. Hats. 2. Caps (Headgear) 3. Knitting--Patterns. 4. Children's clothing. I. Title.

TT825.W37285 2008
746.43'2041--dc22
                                    2008001789

Printed in China
10 9 8 7 6 5 4 3 2 1

*My sisters, Ann and Emily, are the
true writers in my family, so it strikes
me as funny that I am the one who
ended up having my work published.*

*I can always count on getting the same
wonderful reaction whenever I show
either one of them my latest knitting
creation. They hold their heads, much
like our father, Sam, and scream and
laugh with great enthusiasm. Up until
recently I always knew who my biggest
fan was, but now that my father is gone,
that torch has been passed.*

*This book is dedicated with love and
affection to Ann and Emily Milstein,
my two wildly talented sisters, whom
I wildly love.*

Acknowledgments

Thank you to my husband, Will, for cooking the dinners, doing the dishes, running the errands, and holding down the fort while allowing me the luxury of pursuing my talents. And thank you, Owen, for your help in giving a name to all my creations and your never-ending zest. You are simply the best.

I want to thank Pamela Hoenig, who first approached me about this project with The Taunton Press. My thanks also to my editors, Erica Sanders-Foege and Courtney Jordan, who kept things easily organized.

Thanks to James Roderick for taking all the lovely photographs. A special recognition and thank-you to Joann Dilorenzo, stylist extraordinaire, whose talent, efforts, and patience were so appreciated. Thank you, Linda Hall, for the help with the photography and for all your efforts.

For my dear friend Beth Joansen, who spent days with me at the photo shoot wrangling babies, running errands, sleeping on the couch, and doing whatever needed to be done. Somehow, thanking you here, on this page, doesn't seem quite enough. Nevertheless—thank you!

Finally, my special thanks to the knitters and shop owners around the country who have responded so enthusiastically to my baby designs. Your encouragement is so appreciated, and I hope you enjoy knitting these new creations as well. Have fun!

Contents

Humdingers 90

Introduction

W ELCOME TO MY ZANY WORLD OF KNITTING FOR BABIES! It is not just a world of delicate pastel pinks and blues, but also one filled with bright and unusual color combinations. The 30 hat projects in this book include traditional designs with new twists as well as modern shapes that are easy to create.

My mother, Charlotte, taught me how to knit when I was only eight, and it has been my passion ever since. I cannot remember a time since then that I haven't been working on a sweater for myself or a good friend. It took me years to learn to stop

knitting for boyfriends. It always seemed that the romance was finished just when the sweater was. That's why I still haven't made a sweater for my husband, Will!

I find knitting hats for babies to be a particularly satisfying experience. When designing them, I get inspired by so many things—different colors and shapes, a passing glance at some delightful dessert, or even a chicken! Using graph paper and colored pencils to first sketch an idea is probably prudent, but that's just not my style. I start with needles and some wonderful yarn, then jump in full swing and enjoy the ride. I may have an idea of where I want a project to go, but it usually leads me in an entirely different direction. Who would ever guess, for example, that the Baby Chick Cap started out as an attempt to create a princess crown?

Sometimes what ends up on my needles is pretty awful and I start all over again, but that doesn't mean I haven't enjoyed myself along the way, and this method has led me to some great designs. So don't be afraid to use my patterns as a starting point to your own one-of-a-kind creations. Any way you decide to knit them, the hats in this

book will turn out as wearable tokens of affection that the baby you have in mind will love. The projects are so quick to complete that there's no chance of tedium setting in, and unlike socks or gloves, you only need to create one!

Yarns for these projects range from colorful cottons to warm chenilles and soft, glittery nylons. I mostly suggest machine-washable yarns throughout the book, but even in today's busy world, hand-washing a small baby hat is doable. The few novelty yarns I recommend are used repeatedly in my designs, so buy just one skein and you'll be set.

A word about sizing: Babies are born with different size heads, and those head sizes vary even more during the first year. The ages and corresponding hat sizes given here are suggestions. Be sure to measure the head of the baby for whom you are creating these wonderful hats so you can be sure the fit is right. Remember that cotton is a fickle fiber—it tends to resist stretching when used with certain stitches, like Seed stitch. Keep that in mind when sizing your hats.

Homecomings

Glitter & Glow Beanie

This sweet and elegant beanie is a snap to make. Tie it up with a giant fancy ribbon and make a delightful present out of the precious newborn you have in mind!

Sizing

3 to 18 months (16-in. circumference)

Yarn

DK Weight smooth yarn

DK Weight eyelash yarn

The hat shown is made with S.R. Kertzer Super 10 Cotton: 100% mercerized cotton, 4.4 oz. (125 g)/250 yd. (228.6 m) and Stylecraft Icicle: 62% polyester, 38% metallized polyester, 1.75 oz. (50 g)/87 yd. (80 m).

Yardage

50 yd. Super 10 Cotton #3446 Cotton Candy or #3841 Caribbean

30 yd. Super 10 Cotton #3532 Soft Yellow

40 yd. Icicle #1140 Crystal or #1142 Sunlight

Materials

16-in. U.S. size 4 circular needle

1-in.-wide ribbon, 10 in. long

Stitch marker

Tapestry needle

GAUGE

22 sts = 4 in. with Super 10 Cotton

SEED STITCH

Rnd 1: *K1, P1; rep from * to end of rnd.

All other rnds: K the P sts and P the K sts.

Directions

HAT BASE

With circ needles and Cotton Candy/Caribbean, CO 72 sts. Place a st marker on right needle and, beginning Rnd 1, join CO sts together making sure that sts do not become twisted on needle.

Rnd 1: P.

Work Seed st for 4 in.

Drop Cotton Candy/Caribbean and attach Soft
    Yellow. *K1 rnd, P1 rnd. Rep from * once.

STRIPED TOP

Rnd 1: *K2 with Cotton Candy/Caribbean. Drop
    Cotton Candy/Caribbean and, keeping yarn in the
    back of your work, K2 with Soft Yellow; rep from *
    for entire rnd.

Rnd 2: *K2 with Cotton Candy/Caribbean. P2 with
    Soft Yellow; rep from * for entire rnd.

Rep Rnd 2 for 15 rnds.

Next Rnd: Cut Soft Yellow and with Cotton Candy/
    Caribbean, K entire rnd.

Eyelet Rnd: *K1, YO, K2tog, K5; rep from * to end
    of rnd.

Next Rnd: K entire rnd.

Cut Cotton Candy/Caribbean and attach Icicle.
    K1 rnd. P1 rnd.

SQUIGGLES

Step 1: Using the Cable Cast-On (see p. 133),
    CO 6 sts.

Step 2: BO those 6 sts.

Step 3: K6 sts from hat top.

Rep these 3 steps for entire rnd. BO all sts.

FINISHING

Weave in all loose ends. Thread a sweet ribbon
    through the eyelets and tie a big, beautiful bow
    on top of the hat. It'll be an instant sensation!

Birthday Cupcake Cap

This sugar-coated hat is so sweet you'll want to eat it up! With French Knots, you create festive sprinkles, and the candle in the middle has a little glittery flame to help celebrate the special day.

Sizing

Newborn to 1 year (14-in. circumference)

Yarn

DK Weight smooth yarn

DK Weight eyelash yarn

Bulky Weight bouclé yarn

The hat shown is made with S.R. Kertzer
Super 10 Cotton: 100% mercerized cotton,
4.4 oz. (125 g)/250 yd. (228.6 m); Stylecraft
Icicle: 62% polyester, 38% metallized polyester,
1.75 oz. (50 g)/87 yd. (80 m); and Lion Brand
Yarn Homespun®: 98% acrylic, 2% polyester,
6 oz. (170 g)/185 yd./(169 m).

Yardage

60 yd. Super 10 Cotton #3446 Cotton Candy
or #3841 Caribbean

3 yd. Super 10 Cotton #3997 Scarlet

5 yd. Super 10 Cotton White

2 yd. Homespun #790-389 Spring Green

30 yd. Icicle #1143 Sunlight

Materials

16-in. U.S. size 4 circular needle

Four U.S. size 4 double-pointed needles

Stitch marker

Tapestry needle

GAUGE

22 sts = 4 in. with Super 10 Cotton

SEED STITCH

Rnd 1: *K1, P1; rep from * to end of rnd.

All other rnds: K the P sts and P the K sts.

Directions

HAT BASE

With circ needles and Cotton Candy/Caribbean, CO
72 sts. Place a st marker on right needle and,
beginning Rnd 1, join CO sts together making
sure that sts do not become twisted on needle.

Rnd 1: P.

Work Seed st for 3 in.

Cut Cotton Candy/Caribbean and attach
Homespun.

K1 rnd. P1 rnd.

Cut Homespun and attach Icicle.

CROWN

With Icicle, work Seed st on all rnds for approx 2 in.

DECREASE ROUNDS

Dec Rnd 1: *K7, K2tog; rep from * to end of rnd.

Dec Rnd 2: *K6, K2tog; rep from * to end of rnd.

Dec Rnd 3: *K5, K2tog; rep from * to end of rnd.

Continue in established pattern, knitting one less
st between dec and changing to dpns when
necessary. Cut yarn, leaving a 6-in. tail. Using
a tapestry needle, thread the tail through the rem
sts on the needles. Pull the yarn, gathering sts
tightly together, then secure the tail on the WS
of work.

BIRTHDAY CANDLE

With 2 dpns and White, CO 7 sts.

Work I-Cord (see p.134) for 14 rnds.

Cut White, attach Icicle, and work 3 rnds.

Cut Icicle and, using a tapestry needle, thread the
Icicle and White tails through the rem sts on
the needle and pass all tails through the inside
of the I-Cord.

Using those tails, attach the candle securely to the
tip of the hat for a candle that will never burn out!

Make French Knots (see p.134) with Scarlet to
create sprinkles on the top of your cupcake.

WELT

Thread a tapestry needle with White, pinch the hat
at the Homespun pure rnd, and create a Welt
(see p.135) by sewing together the top and
bottom pieces using even running stitches.

FINISHING

Weave in all loose ends. Now it's birthday time!

Baby Beastie Beanie

With a little smirk and sparkling ear tips, this charming hat can be your littlest one's best animal pal. It is so easy and quick to knit that you'll soon have a bunch of beasties at your fingertips!

Sizing

Newborn to 2 years (14-in. circumference)

Yarn

DK Weight smooth yarn

DK Weight eyelash yarn

The hat shown is made with S.R. Kertzer Super 10 Cotton: 100% mercerized cotton, 4.4 oz. (125 g)/250 yd. (228.6 m) and Stylecraft Icicle: 62% polyester, 38% metallized polyester, 1.75 oz. (50 g)/87 yd. (80 m).

Yardage

50 yd. Super 10 Cotton Cream

20 yd. Super 10 Cotton #3446 Cotton Candy or #3841 Caribbean

2 yd. Super 10 Cotton #3722 Celery

3 yd. Icicle #1141 Polar

Materials

16-in. U.S. size 4 circular needle

One pair U.S. size 4 straight needles

Stitch marker

Tapestry needle

GAUGE

22 sts = 4 in. with Super 10 Cotton

Directions

HAT BASE

With circ needles and Cotton Candy/Caribbean, CO 70 sts. Place a st marker on right needle and, beginning Rnd 1, join CO sts together making sure that sts do not become twisted on needle.

Rnd 1: P.

Rnds 2–26: K.

BEASTIE'S EARS

You will divide the work in half and work back and
forth on straight needles—not in the round—for
the remainder of the hat.

Row 1 (RS): K35.

Row 2 (WS): P.

Row 3: K1, sl 1, K1, psso. Work to the last 3 sts.
K2tog, K1.

Rep Rows 2 and 3 until 23 sts rem. P1 row. Cut
Cream and attach Cotton Candy/Caribbean.
Continue dec until 7 sts rem on needle. Attach
Icicle and K only (Garter st) for 1 in. Cut all yarn,
leaving a 6-in. tail. Thread tapestry needle and
pass it through the rem sts on the needle.
Secure to WS of work.

Attach Cream where the work was divided for first
ear and create the second ear following the
same directions.

FINISHING

With Cream, thread a tapestry needle with tails and
sew the Beastie's head closed, using the photo
on the facing page as a reference. The base
of this seam will be where the nose is added.
Weave in all loose ends.

BEASTIE NOSE

With Cotton Candy/Caribbean and straight needles,
CO 1 st. K1f&b 3 times, K1, creating 7 sts from
1 st. Work 5 rows in Garter st.

Dec Row: Sl 1, K1, psso. Work to the last 2 sts
and K2tog. Cut the yarn, leaving a 4-in. tail.
Thread a tapestry needle and pass it through
the rem sts on the needle. Tie CO and BO tails
together to form a ball. Attach this to the Beastie
at the base of the Cream seam. With Cotton
Candy/Caribbean, make 2 French Knots for the
eyes (see p. 134). Using the photograph at left as
a reference, embroider Celery circles around the
eyes. With Cotton Candy/Caribbean, embroider
your own delightful smirk of a smile.

FINAL TOUCH

Using Icicle, make a small French Knot in the middle
of the Beastie's nose for an added touch of fun.

Newborn Beanie

Create this beanie in bright, bold colors or soft pastels. Easy-to-make French Knots add a touch of whimsy. This is the perfect hat for bringing your new sweetie home in style.

Sizing

Newborn to 6 months (14-in. circumference)

Yarn

DK Weight smooth yarn

The hat shown is made with S.R. Kertzer Super
  10 Cotton: 100% mercerized cotton, 4.4 oz.
  (125 g)/250 yd. (228.6 m).

Yardage

Pastel Beanie

60 yd. Super 10 Cotton White

15 yd. Super 10 Cotton #3532 Soft Yellow

5 yd. Super 10 Cotton #3722 Celery

5 yd. Super 10 Cotton #3443 Cotton Candy

5 yd. Super 10 Cotton #3841 Caribbean

Bright Beanie

60 yd. Super 10 Cotton #3553 Canary

15 yd. Super 10 Cotton #3997 Scarlet

5 yd. Super 10 Cotton #3764 Peppermint

5 yd. Super 10 Cotton #3062 Turquoise

Materials

16-in. U.S. size 4 circular needle

Four U.S. size 4 double-pointed needles

Four stitch markers

Tapestry needle

GAUGE

22 sts = 4 in.

Directions

HAT BASE

With circ needles and Soft Yellow/Scarlet, CO
  72 sts. Place a st marker on right needle and,
  beginning Rnd 1, join CO sts together making
  sure that sts do not become twisted on needle.

Note: Always keep unworked yarn on the WS of
  your work and sl sts pw.

Rnd 1: P.

Drop Soft Yellow/Scarlet and attach Caribbean/
  Turquoise.

Cut all yarn and attach White/Canary. K15 rnds.
Drop White/Canary and reattach Soft Yellow/Scarlet.
K1 rnd. P1 rnd.
Rep Rnds 2–5. Substitute White/Canary for Soft
Yellow/Scarlet. Cut Soft Yellow/Scarlet. With
White/Canary, K1 rnd and divide work into
4 sections, placing a st marker after each 18th st.

SWIRL CROWN

At every st marker in each rnd, make the following
dec: Sl marker, sl 1 pw, K1, psso. Move sts
to dpns when necessary. Continue until 3 sts
remain. Drop White/Canary, attach Soft Yellow/
Scarlet and work I-Cord (see p. 134) for 3 in.
Pick up White/Canary and work 1 in. Cut all yarn,
leaving a 6-in. tail. Thread a tapestry needle and
pass it through the remaining sts on the knitting
needle. Pass needle and tails through the center
of the I-Cord into the WS of the crown and
secure.

FINISHING

Weave in all loose ends. Make French Knots (see
p. 134) in Celery, Cotton Candy, and Caribbean
or Scarlet, Peppermint, and Turquoise, using
the photograph on the facing page as a reference. Tie the I-Cord into a knot so that the White/
Canary tip peeks out.

Rnd 2: With Caribbean/Turquoise, *K1, sl 1 st; rep
from * to end of rnd.

Rnd 3: With Caribbean/Turquoise, *P1, sl 1 st; rep
from * to end of rnd.

Rnd 4: Cut Caribbean/Turquoise and pick up Soft
Yellow/Scarlet. K entire rnd.

Rnd 5: With Soft Yellow/Scarlet, P entire rnd.
Rep Rnds 2–5 three times. Substitute Celery/
Canary for Caribbean/Turquoise in first repetition
and Cotton Candy/Peppermint for Celery/Canary
in second repetition.

Greenie Beanie

This tiny beanie with flowers on top is perfect for your tiny one! It is so easy to create that you'll want to knit one in every color of the rainbow.

Sizing

Newborn (13-in. circumference) to 2 years (16-in. circumference)

Figures for larger size are given below in parentheses. Where only one set of figures appears, the directions apply to both sizes.

Yarn

DK Weight smooth yarn

The hat shown is made with S.R. Kertzer Super 10 Cotton: 100% mercerized cotton, 4.4 oz. (125 g)/250 yd. (228.6 m).

Yardage

60 (70) yd. Super 10 Cotton #3722 Celery
Small amount of Super 10 Cotton #3525 Cornsilk
Small amount of Super 10 Cotton #3841 Caribbean
Small amount of Super 10 Cotton #3533 Daffodil

Materials

16-in. U.S. size 4 circular needle
Four U.S. size 4 double-pointed needles
Stitch marker
Tapestry needle

GAUGE

22 sts = 4 in.

SEED STITCH

Rnd 1: *K1, P1; rep from * to end of rnd.
All other rnds: K the P sts and P the K sts.

Directions

HAT BASE

With circ needles and Celery, CO 60 (70) sts. Place a st marker on right needle and, beginning Rnd 1, join CO sts together making sure that sts do not become twisted on needle.

Rnd 1: P.

Work Seed st for 3 1/2 (4) in.

Drop Celery and attach Cornsilk. K1 rnd, P1 rnd.

Cut Cornsilk and pick up Celery. Work Seed st an additional 2 in.

Length of beanie from base should be 6 (7) in. Cut yarn, leaving an 8-in. tail. Using a tapestry needle, thread the tail through all the sts on the needle. Pull the yarn, gathering the sts tightly together, then secure the tail on the WS of the beanie.

STEMS

With Caribbean, CO 6 sts and work I-Cord (see p. 134) for 20 rows.
Make 2 I-Cords.

LEAVES

With Celery and 2 dpns, CO 4 sts. K1 row. At beg of each following row, K1, Kf&b, K across until you have 8 sts. K1 row. At beg of each following row, K2tog, K across until 4 sts rem.
BO all sts.
Make 2 leaves.

FLOWERS

With Daffodil and 2 dpns, CO 14 sts. Kf&b into each st. BO pw. Curl into a flower.
Make 2 flowers.

FINISHING

Sew the stems onto the top of the hat. Attach a leaf to each one, then attach the flower to the top. Weave in all loose ends.

Fancy Scrumptious Beanie

Worked in Seed stitch, this pastel jewel of a beanie is a sweet choice for baby's homecoming. Finger toppers add just the right amount of playfulness.

Sizing

Newborn (12-in. circumference) to 6 months (14-in. circumference)

Figures for larger size are given below in parentheses. Where only one set of figures appears, the directions apply to both sizes.

Yarn

DK Weight smooth yarn

The hat shown is made with S.R. Kertzer Super 10 Cotton: 100% mercerized cotton, 4.4 oz. (125 g)/250 yd. (228.6 m) and Super 10 Cotton Multi: 100% mercerized cotton, 3.5 oz. (100 g)/220 yd. (201 m).

Yardage

30 (35) yd. Super 10 Cotton White

40 (55) yd. Super 10 Cotton Multi #2015 Early Spring

Materials

16-in. U.S. size 4 circular needle

Four U.S. size 4 double-pointed needles

Stitch marker

Tapestry needle

GAUGE

22 sts = 4 in.

SEED STITCH

Rnd 1: *K1, P1; rep from * to end of rnd.

All other rnds: K the P sts and P the K sts.

Directions

HAT BASE

With circ needles and White, CO 81 (99) sts. Place a st marker on right needle and, beginning Rnd 1, join CO sts together making sure that sts do not become twisted on needle.

Note: Always keep unworked yarn on the WS of your work and sl sts pw.

Rnd 1: P.

FIRST TIER

Rnd 1: Attach Multi. *K1 with White, K1 with Multi; rep from * to end of rnd.

Rnd 2: Drop White. *Sl 1 wyib (White st), P1 with Multi; rep from * to end of rnd.

Rnd 3: *K1 with White, P1 with Multi; rep from * to end of rnd.

Rnds 4 & 5: Rep Rnd 3.

Rnd 6: K with White.

Rnd 7: P with White.

SECOND TIER

Rnd 1: *K1 with Multi, K1 with White; rep from * to end of rnd.

Rnd 2: Drop Multi. *Sl 1 wyib (Multi st), P1 with White; rep from * to end of rnd.

Rnd 3: *P1 with Multi, K1 with White; rep from * to end of rnd.

Rnds 4 & 5: Rep Rnd 3.

Rnd 6: K with White.

Rnd 7: P with White.

THIRD TIER

Rep First Tier rnds.

Cut White and with Multi, K1 rnd, then work Seed st for 3 (4) in.

DECREASE ROUNDS

Dec Rnd 1: *K7, K2tog; rep from * to end of rnd.

Dec Rnd 2: *K6, K2tog; rep from * to end of rnd.

Continue in established dec pattern, knitting 1 less st between dec and switching to dpns when necessary until 5 sts rem.

FINGER TOPPERS

Using the Cable Cast-On (see p. 133), CO 5 sts. BO those 5 sts. Rep for entire rnd. Cut yarn, leaving a 6-in. tail. Thread tapestry needle and pass the yarn through the rem sts on needle. Secure to WS of work.

CREATE WELT

Thread a tapestry needle with White, pinch the hat at the last White pure rnd, and create a Welt (see p. 135) by sewing together the top and bottom pieces using even running stitches. Pull slightly on White yarn to create a pucker effect that makes the crown flow over the top tier. Weave in all loose ends.

Rainbow Sack Hat

This cheery and colorful hat knits straight up. All you have to do is make a large bow at the top to cinch the sack.

Sizing

Newborn (12-in. circumference) to 18 months (16-in. circumference)

Figures for larger size are given below in parentheses. Where only one set of figures appears, the directions apply to both sizes.

Yarn

DK Weight smooth yarn

The hat shown is made with S.R. Kertzer Super 10 Cotton: 100% mercerized cotton, 4.4 oz. (125 g)/250 yd. (228.6 m) and Super 10 Cotton Multi: 100% mercerized cotton, 3.5 oz. (100 g)/ 220 yd. (201 m).

Yardage

60 yd. Super 10 Cotton Multi #2016 Carousel

30 yd. Super 10 Cotton #3997 Scarlet

30 yd. Super 10 Cotton White

Materials

16-in. U.S. size 4 circular needle

Two U.S. size 4 double-pointed needles

Stitch marker

Tapestry needle

GAUGE

22 sts = 4 in.

SEED STITCH

Rnd 1: *K1, P1; rep from * to end of rnd.

All other rnds: K the P sts and P the K sts.

Directions

HAT BASE

With circ needles and Scarlet, CO 60 (88) sts. Place a st marker on right needle and, beginning Rnd 1, join CO sts together making sure that sts do not become twisted on needle.

Note: Always keep unworked yarn on the WS of your work and sl sts pw.

Rnd 1: P.

Rnd 2: Drop Scarlet and attach Multi. With Multi *K1, sl 1 wyib; rep from * to end of rnd.

Rnd 3: With Multi *P1, sl 1 wyib; rep from * to end of rnd.

Rnd 4: Drop Multi, pick up Scarlet, and K entire rnd.

Rnd 5: P entire rnd with Scarlet.

Rep Rnds 2–5 four times (a total of 5 repetitions).

Cut Scarlet and K1 rnd with Multi. Work Seed st for 3 (4) in.

Attach Scarlet and K1 rnd. Work K1, P1 ribbing for 2 rnds.

EYELET ROUND

*K4, YO, K2tog. Work established ribbing for 8 sts; rep from * to last K2tog; end K4.

Continue with established ribbing for a total of 14 rnds. BO all sts.

FINISHING

Using dpns and White, CO 3 sts. Work I-Cord (see p. 134) for desired length to create a big bow. Weave in loose ends and work I-Cord through eyelets. Draw top of hat closed and tie bow.

Hobo Hat

With small patches and a Pom Pom, your little hobo will be ready to go adventuring in this adorable cap, brimmed in Seed stitch.

Sizing

Newborn (15-in. circumference) to 18 months (17-in. circumference)

Figures for larger size are given below in parentheses. Where only one set of figures appears, the directions apply to both sizes.

Yarn

DK Weight smooth yarn

The hat shown is made with S.R. Kertzer Super 10 Cotton: 100% mercerized cotton, 4.4 oz. (125 g)/250 yd. (228.6 m).

Yardage

70 (80) yd. Super 10 Cotton #3882 Periwinkle

Small amount of Super 10 Cotton #3724 Lime

Small amount of Super 10 Cotton #3997 Scarlet

Small amount of Super 10 Cotton #3553 Canary

Materials

16-in. U.S. size 4 circular needle

Four U.S. size 4 double-pointed needles

One pair U.S. size 4 straight needles

Stitch marker

Tapestry needle

Pom Pom maker (1½ in.)

GAUGE

22 sts = 4 in.

SEED STITCH

Rnd 1: *K1, P1; rep from * to end of rnd.

All other rnds: K the P sts and P the K sts.

Directions

HAT BASE

With circ needles and Periwinkle, CO 72 (88) sts.
Place a st marker on right needle and, beginning Rnd 1, join CO sts together making sure that sts do not become twisted on needle.

Rnd 1: P.

Work Seed st for 1½ in.

K10 (15) rnds.

DECREASE ROUNDS

Dec Rnd 1: *K7 (6), K2tog; rep from * for entire rnd. K9 rnds.

Dec Rnd 2: *K6 (5), K2tog; rep from * for entire rnd. K5 rnds.

Rep decs as established, knitting 1 less st between dec for each rnd and knitting 5 rnds between each dec rnd, putting sts on dpns when necessary. When you have approx 4–7 sts on the needle, cut the yarn, leaving a 6-in. tail. Using a tapestry needle, thread the tail through the remaining sts on the needles. Pull the yarn, gathering sts tightly together, then secure the tail on the WS of the crown.

PATCHES

Make 2 (3) patches each of Canary, Lime, and Scarlet for a total of 6 (9) patches.

CO 3 sts using straight needles.

Row 1 (RS): K1f&b, K1, K1f&b—5 sts.

Row 2 (WS): P.

Row 3: K1f&b, K to last st, K1f&b.

Row 4: P.

Row 5: K to last st, K1f&b.

Row 6: P.

Rep Rows 5 & 6 until you have 10 sts.

Next Row (RS): Sl 1, K1, psso, K6, K2tog.

Next Row (WS): P.

Next Row (RS): K to last st, K2tog.

Next Row (WS): P.

Rep the last 2 rows until 3 sts rem. BO these 3 sts, leaving a 12-in. tail.

Thread a tapestry needle with the tail and weave yarn through sts on WS of patch.

FINISHING

Weave in all loose ends. Thread a tapestry needle with Periwinkle and whipstitch the patches all around the hat. Using contrasting colors, make French Knots (see p. 134) in the center of each patch. Finally, make a 1$\frac{1}{2}$-in. Pom Pom (see p. 135) with Canary, Lime, Scarlet, and Periwinkle and sew it onto the tip of the hat. Your Hobo Hat is now ready for your little hobo!

Baby Chick Cap

Here, chick, chick! A sweet, fluffy chick sitting in its own basket among the grass—what could be a more perfect hat for your little newborn?

Sizing

Newborn to 18 months (14-in. circumference)

Yarn

DK Weight smooth yarn

DK Weight eyelash yarn

The hat shown is made with S.R. Kertzer Super 10 Cotton: 100% mercerized cotton, 4.4 oz. (125 g)/ 250 yd. (228.6 m) and Stylecraft Icicle: 62% polyester, 38% metallized polyester, 1.75 oz. (50 g)/87 yd. (80 m).

Yardage

60 yd. Super 10 Cotton #3223 Tan

30 yd. Super 10 Cotton #3841 Caribbean or #3446 Cotton Candy

25 yd. Super 10 Cotton #3722 Celery

1 yd. Super 10 Cotton #3997 Scarlet

1 yd. Super 10 Cotton Black

50 yd. Icicle #1142 Sunlight

Materials

16-in. U.S. size 4 circular needle

One pair U.S. size 4 straight needles

Stitch marker

Tapestry needle

GAUGE

22 sts = 4 in. with Super 10 Cotton

SEED STITCH

Rnd 1: *K1, P1; rep from * to end of rnd.

All other rnds: K the P sts and P the K sts.

Directions

HAT BASE

With circ needles and Tan, CO 72 sts. Place a st marker on right needle and, beginning Rnd 1, join CO sts together making sure that sts do not become twisted on needle.

Note: Always keep unworked yarn on the WS of your work and sl sts pw.

Rnd 1: P. Drop Tan and attach Caribbean/Cotton
Candy.

Rnd 2: *K1, sl 1 st with Caribbean/Cotton Candy;
rep from * to end of rnd.

Rnd 3: *P1, sl 1 st with Caribbean/Cotton Candy;
rep from * to end of rnd.

Rnd 4: Drop Caribbean/Cotton Candy and pick up
Tan. K entire rnd.

Rnd 5: P with Tan.

Rep Rnds 2–5 eight times. Cut all yarn. Attach
Celery.

GRASS

Using the Cable Cast-On (see p. 133), create
blades of grass that alternate in length from 6 sts
long to 8 sts long as follows: With Celery, *CO
6 sts, BO those 6 sts, K1, CO 8 sts, BO those
8 sts, K1. Rep from * for the entire rnd. K1 rnd
with Celery.

CHICK

Cut Celery and attach Icicle. You will divide the
work in half and work back and forth on straight
needles—not in the round—for the remainder
of the hat.

Row 1: K36 with Icicle.

Work in Seed st for 2 1/2 in. BO all sts and cut the
yarn, leaving a 10-in. tail.

Attach Icicle on RS where the work was divided for
the first half. K1 row. Work back and forth in
Seed st for 2 1/2 in.

Dec Rows: K2tog 5 times at beg of the next
2 rows.

Next Dec Rows: K2tog at the beg and end
of each row 4 times until you have 22 sts on
the needle.

Cut the yarn, leaving a 10-in. tail. Thread a tapestry
needle and pass it through the rem sts on
the needle. Pull tightly and—presto!—the head
of the chick takes shape. With the same tail,
sew a seam along the top of the chick and
secure the remainder of the yarn to the inside of
the work. With the other tail, carefully sew up the
width of the chick.

FINISHING

Weave in all loose ends. With Black, make two
French Knots (see p. 134) for the eyes of the
chick. Make a large French Knot using Scarlet for
the beak. This cute chick cap is complete!

Hooplas

Halloween Hat

Whose little pumpkin wouldn't love this little pumpkin hat? The eyes and mouth are made with Duplicate Stitch, so create any expression you want on this trick-or-treat topper.

Sizing

Newborn (14-in. circumference) to 12 months (16-in. circumference)

Figures for larger size are given below in parentheses. Where only one set of figures appears, the directions apply to both sizes.

Yarn

DK Weight smooth yarn

The hat shown is made with S.R. Kertzer Super 10 Cotton: 100% mercerized cotton, 4.4 oz. (125 g)/250 yd. (228.6 m).

Yardage

70 (80) yd. Super 10 Cotton #3402 Nectarine

30 (40) yd. Super 10 Cotton #3764 Peppermint

10 yd. Super 10 Cotton #3553 Canary

2 yd. Super 10 Cotton #3327 Chocolate

Materials

16-in. U.S. size 3 circular needle

Four U.S. size 3 double-pointed needles

11 stitch markers

Tapestry needle

GAUGE

22 sts = 4 in.

Directions

HAT BASE

With circ needle and Peppermint, CO 74 (88) sts. Place a st marker on right needle and, beginning Rnd 1, join CO sts together making sure that sts do not become twisted on needle.

Note: Always keep the unworked yarn on the WS of the work and sl sts pw.

Rnd 1: P.

Rnd 2: Drop Peppermint and attach Nectarine. With Nectarine *K1, sl 1 wyib; rep from * to end of rnd.

Rnd 3: With Nectarine *P1, sl 1 wyib; rep from * to end of rnd.

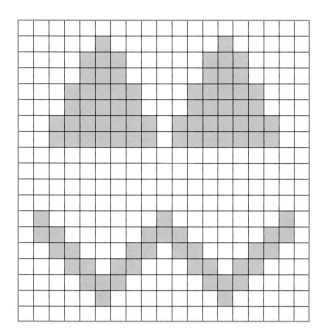

HALLOWEEN HAT CHART • Use Canary to Duplicate Stitch a friendly face onto your pumpkin hat.

Rnd 4: Drop Nectarine. K entire rnd with Peppermint.

Rnd 5: P with Peppermint.

Rep Rnds 2–5 twice (3 repetitions total).

INCREASE ROUND

Cut Peppermint and pick up Nectarine.

Inc Rnd 1: Smaller size: *K1, K1f&b; rep from * to last 2 sts; K2. Larger size: *K1, K1f&b; rep from* for entire rnd. There should be 110 (132) sts on the needle.

RIBBING PATTERN

With Nectarine *K9 (11), P1; rep from * for entire rnd. Continue with this ribbing pattern for 20 (25) rnds.

RIDGE ROUND

Drop Nectarine and attach Peppermint. K1 rnd. P1 rnd. Drop Peppermint, and with Nectarine work Ribbing Pattern for 6 (8) rnds. Drop Nectarine and attach Peppermint. K1 rnd. P1 rnd.

SWIRL TOP

Drop Peppermint and attach Nectarine. K entire rnd, placing a st marker every 10 (12) sts (after P st of ribbing). For 6 rnds, make the following dec at each marker: Sl marker, sl 1 st, K1 st, psso. Drop Nectarine and attach Peppermint. K1 rnd. P1 rnd. Cut Peppermint and attach Nectarine. K2tog for the entire rnd until about 4–5 sts rem. Cut Nectarine and attach Chocolate. Work an I-Cord (see p. 134) for approx 10 rnds or until you have the desired length of stem for your pumpkin. Cut the yarn, leaving a 6-in. tail. Using a tapestry needle, thread the tail through the remaining sts on the needle. Bring yarn through the I-Cord to the WS of the work.

FINISHING

Weave in all ends. Using Duplicate Stitch (see p.133) and Canary, embroider a friendly or ghoulish face onto your pumpkin as shown on the facing page and using the chart above or your own design. Using Nectarine, make French Knots (see p. 134) for bright eyes.

Glittery Holiday Hat

For the baby who wants to shine! This sparkling hat has a festive holiday flower on the tip for a little extra glitz.

Sizing

6 months (16-in. circumference) to 2 years (18-in. circumference)

Figures for larger size are given below in parentheses. Where only one set of figures appears, the directions apply to both sizes.

Yarn

DK Weight smooth yarn

DK Weight eyelash yarn

The hat shown is made with S.R. Kertzer Super 10 Cotton: 100% mercerized cotton, 4.4 oz. (125 g)/250 yd. (228.6 m) and Stylecraft Icicle: 62% polyester, 38% metallized polyester, 1.75 oz. (50 g)/87 yd. (80 m).

Yardage

25 yd. Super 10 Cotton #3997 Scarlet

60 yd. Super 10 Cotton #3764 Peppermint

30 yd. Super 10 Cotton #3062 Turquoise

10 yd. Icicle #1141 Polar

Materials

16-in. U.S. size 4 circular needle

Four U.S. size 4 double-pointed needles

Stitch marker

Tapestry needle

GAUGE

22 sts = 4 in. with Super 10 Cotton

Directions

HAT BASE

With circ needles and Peppermint, CO 81 (99). Place a st marker on right needle and, beginning Rnd 1, join CO sts together making sure that sts do not become twisted on needle.

Rnd 1: P.

Rnds 2–13: K.

Drop Peppermint. Attach Turquoise and begin pattern for Ridge Stripes.

RIDGE STRIPES

Rnd 1: With Turquoise, K.

Rnd 2: P.

Drop Turquoise. Pick up Peppermint and **K5 rnds. Drop Peppermint, pick up Turquoise. K1 rnd, making the following decs on that rnd: *K7, K2tog; rep from * for entire rnd.

Next Rnd: P with Turquoise. Drop Turquoise. Pick up Peppermint and rep from **.

Continue in established pattern, knitting 1 less st between decs and switching to dpns when necessary, until you have completed the 9th Turquoise ridge. Work an I-Cord (see p. 134) with rem sts for about 2 in.

Cut yarn and thread a tapestry needle. Pass the tapestry needle through the rem sts on needle. Then pass the needle through the center of the I-Cord, pulling securely to gather the I-Cord into a little squiggle.

HOLIDAY FLOWER

With 2 dpns and Scarlet, CO 10 sts.

Row 1 (RS): K.

Row 2 (and all even rows): P.

Row 3: K1f&b of each st—20 sts.

Row 5: K1f&b of each st—40 sts.

Cut Scarlet and attach Icicle.

Row 6: P.

BO all sts.

FINISHING

Weave in all loose ends on hat and flower. Thread a tapestry needle with Scarlet and, using Duplicate Stitch (see p. 133), create zigzags on the second Peppermint band, which will end up being the bottom band of the hat.

Thread a tapestry needle with Peppermint and fold the first Peppermint band inside the hat, so that the Turquoise ridge becomes the rim of the hat. Sew the band to the inside of the hat. Curl your Holiday Flower into a tight spiral and, with CO tail, attach the flower to I-Cord. Make a Turquoise French Knot (see p. 134) in the center of the flower.

Thread a tapestry needle with Icicle and create more French Knots along the ridge of the hat directly above the Scarlet zigzags. Happy Holidays!

Tea Garden Hat

Think tea parties in spring! Chenille gives a touch of elegance to this hat—perfect for the little girl who loves playing dress-up.

Sizing

6 to 18 months (14-in. circumference)

Yarn

DK Weight smooth yarn

Bulky Weight chenille yarn

Worsted Weight ribbon yarn

The hat shown is made with S.R. Kertzer Super 10 Cotton: 100% mercerized cotton, 4.4 oz. (125 g)/250 yd. (228.6 m); Lion Brand Yarn Chenille Thick & Quick®: 91% acrylic, 9% rayon, 100 yd. (91 m); and Trendsetter Yarns Monarch: 53% nylon, 47% acrylic, 1.75 oz. (50 g)/60 yd. (55 m).

Yardage

30 yd. Super 10 Cotton #3712 Hazel

10 yd. Super 10 Cotton #3936 Wisteria

2 yd. Super 10 Cotton #3402 Nectarine

20 yd. Chenille Thick & Quick #950-178 Basil

20 yd. Monarch #10 Forest Heather

Materials

16-in. U.S. size 4 circular needle

16-in. U.S. size 9 circular needle

Four U.S. size 4 double-pointed needles

Stitch marker

Tapestry needle

GAUGE

22 sts = 4 in. with Super 10 Cotton and size 4 needle

Directions

HAT BASE

With the size 9 circ needle and Chenille, loosely cast on 60 sts. Place a st marker on right needle and, beginning Rnd 1, join CO sts together making sure sts do not become twisted on needle.

Rnd 1: P.

Rnd 2: K.

Rnd 3: P.

Rnd 4: K.

Rnd 5: P.

Cut Chenille and attach Hazel. K next rnd, with the size 4 circ needle. Remember to K this first rnd tightly. After all the sts are on the size 4 circ needle, K15 rnds.

Next Rnd: Drop Hazel and attach Chenille. K next rnd, with the size 9 circ needle. P next rnd.

RIDGE ROUNDS

Drop Chenille. Attach Monarch. K next rnd, with the size 4 circ needle. P next rnd.

*Drop Monarch, pick up Hazel, and K4 rnds. Drop Hazel and pick up Monarch. K1 rnd, P1 rnd. Rep from *.

You will have 2 bands of Hazel and 3 ridges of Monarch. Cut Hazel and Monarch. Attach Wisteria and K1 rnd, putting the sts on dpns.

DECREASE ROUNDS

Dec Rnd 1: *K4, K2tog; rep from * to end of rnd.

Dec Rnd 2: *K3, K2tog; rep from * to end of rnd.

Continue in established pattern, knitting 1 less st between decs until 5–6 sts are on needle.

Cut Wisteria and attach Chenille. Loosely work I-Cord (see p. 134) for 3 rnds. BO.

FINISHING

Weave in all loose ends. Thread a tapestry needle with Wisteria and, using Duplicate Stitch (see p. 133) and the photograph above as a visual reference, embroider diagonal lines around base of hat. Use Nectarine to make French Knots (see p. 134) at the upper end of each line.

Holly Holiday Hat

This seasonal sensation with giant holly leaves and bright red berries will help any little one get into the swing of the holidays!

Sizing

Newborn (14-in. circumference) to 2 years (18-in. circumference)

Figures for larger size are given below in parentheses. Where only one set of figures appears, the directions apply to both sizes.

Yarn

DK Weight smooth yarn

The hat shown is made with S.R. Kertzer Super 10 Cotton: 100% mercerized cotton, 4.4 oz. (125 g)/ 250 yd. (228.6 m).

Yardage

50 (70) yd. Super 10 Cotton #3997 Scarlet

40 (50) yd. Super 10 Cotton #3532 Soft Yellow

60 yd. Super 10 Cotton #3764 Peppermint

Materials

16-in. U.S. size 4 circular needle

Four U.S. size 4 double-pointed needles

One pair U.S. size 4 straight needles

Stitch marker

Tapestry needle

GAUGE

22 sts = 4 in.

SEED STITCH

Rnd 1: *K1, P1; rep from * to end of rnd.

All other rnds: K the P sts and P the K sts.

Directions

HAT BASE

With circ needles and Scarlet, CO 72 (100) sts. Place a st marker on right needle and, beginning Rnd 1, join CO sts together making sure that sts do not become twisted on needle.

Note: Always keep the unworked yarn on the WS of the work and sl sts pw.

Rnd 1: P.

Rnd 2: Drop Scarlet and attach Peppermint. With Peppermint *K1, sl 1 wyib; rep from * to end of rnd.

Rnd 3: With Peppermint *P1, sl 1 wyib; rep from *
to end of rnd.

Rnd 4: Drop Peppermint. K entire rnd with Scarlet.

Rnd 5: P with Scarlet.

Rnds 6–13: Rep Rnds 2–5 two (3) times for a total
of 3 (4) repetitions.

Cut Peppermint and work Seed st with Scarlet for
1 1/2 (2 1/2) in.

Cut Scarlet and attach Peppermint. K1 rnd. P1 rnd.

Cut Peppermint and attach Soft Yellow.
K9 (15) rnds.

DECREASE ROUNDS

Dec Rnd 1: *K7 (8), K2tog; rep from * to end
of rnd.

Dec Rnd 2: *K6 (7), K2tog; rep from * to end
of rnd.

Continue in established pattern, knitting 1 less st
    between decs until you have approx 4–6 sts
    on the needle. Cut the yarn, leaving a 6-in. tail.
    Thread a tapestry needle and pass it through the
    remaining sts on the needle. Bring the tail to the
    WS of the work.

HOLLY LEAVES

With straight needles and Peppermint, CO 5 sts.
    K1 row, P1 row.

Row 1 (RS): *K1f&b, YO, K1, YO, K1, YO,
    K2—9 sts.

Rows 2, 4, 6, 10, 12, 16, and 18: P.

Rows 3 & 9: K4, YO, K1, YO, K4—11 sts.

Rows 5 & 11: K5, YO, K1, YO, K5—13 sts.

Row 7: BO 3 sts, K2, YO, K1, YO, K6—12 sts.

Row 8: BO 3 sts, P8—9 sts.

Row 13: BO 3 sts, K9—10 sts.

Row 14: BO 3 sts, P6—7 sts.

Row 15: Sl 1, K1, psso, K3, K2tog—5 sts.

Row 17: Sl 1, K1, psso, K1, K2tog—3 sts.

Row 18: BO all sts.

Make 6 leaves.

Sew 2 leaves together (WS facing in) to make
    1 fat leaf. You will have 3 fat leaves. Carefully
    sew each leaf base to the tip of the hat.

HOLLY BERRIES

With straight needles and Scarlet, CO 1 st. K1f&b
    3 times, creating 6 sts. Turn.

Rows 1 & 3: K.

Row 2: P.

Row 4: P2tog, P2tog, P2tog—3 sts.

Row 5: K.

Row 6: P3tog. BO.

Knot CO and BO tails together to make the berry.
    Use the tails to attach the berries to the center
    of the hat.

Make 3 berries.

FINISHING

Weave in all loose ends. Thread a tapestry needle
    with Scarlet and use Duplicate Stitch (see
    p. 133) to decorate the first row of Soft Yellow
    at the bottom of the crown. See the photograph
    on the facing page for visual reference. Your Holly
    Holiday Hat is ready for the holidays!

Black and White and Red All Over

This quick-knit hat will be an instant hit with your little one! Red I-Cord and easy-to-find feathers add a big dose of fun.

Sizing

6 months (14-in. circumference) to 2 years (16-in. circumference)

Figures for larger size are given below in parentheses. Where only one set of figures appears, the directions apply to both sizes.

Yarn

DK Weight smooth yarn

The hat shown is made with S.R. Kertzer Super 10 Cotton: 100% mercerized cotton, 4.4 oz. (125 g)/250 yd. (228.6 m).

Yardage

50 (60) yd. Super 10 Cotton White

20 (30) yd. Super 10 Cotton Black

40 (50) yd. Super 10 Cotton #3997 Scarlet

Materials

16-in. U.S. size 4 circular needle

Four U.S. size 4 double-pointed needles

Stitch marker

Tapestry needle

Novelty feathers (from any craft store)

GAUGE

22 sts = 4 in.

Directions

HAT BASE

With circ needles and Black, CO 84 (96) sts. Place a st marker on right needle and, beginning Rnd 1, join CO sts together making sure that sts do not become twisted on needle.

Note: Always keep unworked yarn on the WS of your work and sl sts pw.

Rnd 1: P.

Rnd 2: Attach White. *K1 with White, K1 with Black; rep from * to end of rnd.

Rnd 3: Drop Black. *K1 with White, sl 1 (Black st); rep from * to end of rnd.

Rnd 4: *K1 with White, P1 with Black. Rep from * to end of rnd.

Rnds 5 & 6 (5, 6 & 7): Rep Rnd 4.

Next Rnd: K with Black.

Next Rnd: P with Black.

Cut Black, and with White K7 (8) rnds.

BOBBLE ROUND

Attach Scarlet. *MB (see p. 133 for Bobble instructions), K3; rep from * to end of rnd. Cut Scarlet, and with White K5 (6) rnds.

FINGER ROUND

*With Scarlet, use the Cable Cast-On (see p. 133) to make 8 st. BO all 8 sts. With White K5; rep from * to end of rnd.

Cut Scarlet. With White K1 (2) rnd(s).

CROWN DECREASE ROUNDS

Put sts on dpns when necessary.

Dec Rnd 1: *K10, K2tog; rep from * to end of rnd.

Dec Rnd 2: *K9, K2tog; rep from * to end of rnd.

Continue in established pattern, knitting 1 less st between dec until you have completed 2 rnds of K2tog and have approx 5–7 sts rem on needles. Cut yarn, leaving an 8-in. tail. Thread a tapestry needle with the tail and pass it through rem sts on needle. Before closing the top of the hat, insert feather "base" into hole. Pull tightly and wrap yarn securely around feathers, bringing yarn to the WS of the crown.

I-CORD

CO 3 sts using 2 dpns and Scarlet. Work I-Cord (see p. 134) until I-Cord is long enough to go around the hat. Make 2 I-Cords.

Sew the first I-Cord onto the base of the hat above the Black band. Sew the second above the bobbles, making sure to place it so that the bobbles are centered between the 2 I-Cords.

WELT

Thread a tapestry needle with Black, pinch the hat at the second I-Cord, and create a Welt (see p.135) by sewing together the top and bottom pieces using even running stitches. Pull gently to gather slightly.

Weave in all loose ends.

Crystal Party Hat

This shimmery, iridescent hat is sure to shine all day and night. Knit it up in daffodil yellow or girly girl pink.

Sizing

6 months to 2 years (15-in. circumference)

Yarn

DK Weight smooth yarn

DK Weight eyelash yarn

DK Weight tufted yarn

The hat shown is made with S.R. Kertzer Super 10 Cotton: 100% mercerized cotton, 4.4 oz. (125 g)/250 yd. (228.6 m); Stylecraft Icicle: 62% polyester, 38% metallized polyester, 1.75 oz. (50 g)/87 yd. (80 m); and Stylecraft Marrakech: 79% nylon, 21% acrylic, 1.75 oz. (50 g)/109 yd. (100 m).

Yardage

50 yd. Super 10 Cotton #3533 Daffodil or #3446 Cotton Candy

50 yd. Icicle #1142 Sunlight

30 yd. Marrakech #1158 Seaspray

Materials

16-in. U.S. size 4 circular needle

Four U.S. size 4 double-pointed needles

Stitch marker

Tapestry needle

GAUGE

22 sts = 4 in. with Super 10 Cotton

Directions

HAT BASE

With circ needles and Icicle, CO 72 sts. Place a st marker on right needle and, beginning Rnd 1, join CO sts together making sure sts do not become twisted on needle.

Rnd 1: P.

Rnd 2: K.

Rep Rnds 1 and 2 until work measures approx 1 1/2 in.

FIRST RIDGE ROUND

Drop Icicle and attach Marrakech.

Rnd 1: K.

Rnd 2: P.

Drop Marrakech and pick up Icicle.

Rnd 3: K.

Rnd 4: P.

Drop Icicle and attach Daffodil/Cotton Candy.

Rnd 5: K.

FIRST DECREASE ROUND

Dec Rnd 1: *With Daffodil/Cotton Candy *K7, K2tog; rep from * to end of rnd.

K3 rnds.

SECOND RIDGE ROUND

**Drop Daffodil/Cotton Candy and pick up Icicle.

Rnd 1: K.

Rnd 2: P.

Drop Icicle and pick up Marrakech.

Rnd 3: K.

Rnd 4: P.

Drop Marrakech and pick up Icicle.

Rnd 5: K.

Rnd 6: P.

Drop Icicle and pick up Daffodil/Cotton Candy.

Rnd 7: K.

SECOND DECREASE ROUND

Dec Rnd 1: *With Daffodil/Cotton Candy *K6, K2tog; rep from * to end of rnd.

K3 rnds.

Rep from ** for remainder of hat.

Continue in established pattern, knitting 1 less st

between decs until you have completed the dec rnd of K2, K2tog. You should have a total of 7 Ridge Rounds.

With Daffodil/Cotton Candy, K2tog for an entire rnd until 6 sts rem. Cut Daffodil/Cotton Candy and Icicle. With Marrakech, make an I-Cord (see p. 134) approx 6 in. long.

Cut Marrakech, attach Icicle, and continue I-Cord for 1 in. Cut yarn leaving a 6-in. tail. Use a tapestry needle to draw tail through the remaining sts, then down into the center of the cord.

FINISHING

Weave in all loose ends. Make a knot with the I-Cord and make sure the Icicle tip peeks out to glow and glisten on top!

Fizzle Ruffle Beanie

Ruffles are an easy way to make any hat a fancy hat. This luscious multi-colored beanie is perfect for play dates, parties, and more.

Sizing

3 months (14-in. circumference) to 2 years (16-in. circumference)

Figures for larger size are given below in parentheses. Where only one set of figures appears, the directions apply to both sizes.

Yarn

DK Weight smooth yarn
DK Weight eyelash yarn

The hat shown is made with S.R. Kertzer Super 10 Cotton: 100% mercerized cotton, 4.4 oz. (125 g)/250 yd. (228.6 m); S.R. Kertzer Super 10 Cotton Multi: 100% mercerized cotton, 3.5 oz. (100 g)/220 yd. (201 m); and Trendsetter Yarns Aura: 100% nylon, 1.75 oz. (50 g)/145 yd. (133 m).

Yardage

70 (80) yd. Super 10 Cotton Multi #0494 Orange
40 (50) yd. Super 10 Cotton #3525 Cornsilk
30 yd. Aura #5 Autumn Leaves

Materials

16-in. U.S. size 4 circular needle
Four U.S. size 4 double-pointed needles
Stitch marker
Tapestry needle

GAUGE

22 sts = 4 in. with Super 10 Cotton

SEED STITCH

Rnd 1: *K1, P1; rep from * to end of rnd.
All other rnds: K the P sts and P the K sts.

Directions

HAT BASE

With circ needles and Multi, CO 72 (80) sts. Place a st marker on right needle and, beginning Rnd 1, join CO sts together making sure that sts do not become twisted on needle.

Rnd 1: P.

Work Seed st for 3 (3½) in.

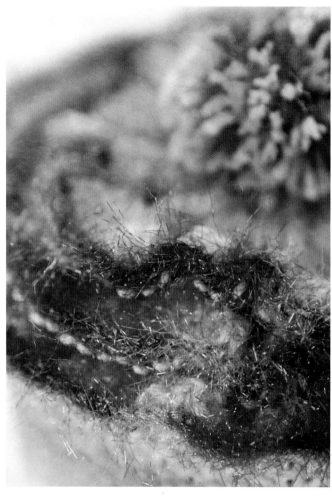

With the RS of the hat facing you, bend the ruffle down toward you and expose the join between the bottom of the ruffle and the top of the Multi Seed st. With Multi, pick up and K1 st in each "upward" loop at this join. There should be 72 (80) sts. K with Multi for 4 rnds.

Rep from * until you have made 3 (4) ruffles.

After picking up the final 72 (80) sts, begin the dec rnds, putting sts on dpns when necessary.

DECREASE ROUNDS

Dec Rnd 1: *K7 (8) K2tog; rep from * to end of rnd.

Dec Rnd 2: *K6 (7) K2tog; rep from * to end of rnd.

Continue in established pattern, knitting 1 less st between decs until you have 4–6 sts on the needle. Cut the yarn, leaving a 6-in. tail. Using a tapestry needle, thread the tail through the remaining sts on the needles. Pull the yarn, gathering the sts tightly together, then secure the tail on the WS of the beanie.

RUFFLE

*Cut Multi and attach Cornsilk.

Rnd 1: K1f&b into every st. There should be 144 (160) sts on the needle. Work Seed st for 4 rnds. Cut Cornsilk and attach Aura. P1 rnd. BO all sts kw.

FINISHING

Weave in all loose ends. Make a Pom Pom (see p. 135) using Multi, Cornsilk, and Aura. Attach it to the top of the hat.

Pretty-in-Pink Cap

This delectable hat takes the cake! Giant yellow bobbles and swirling minty-green "icing" make it absolutely irresistible!

Sizing

3 months to 1 year (15-in. circumference)

Yarn

DK Weight smooth yarn

Worsted Weight ribbon yarn

Bulky Weight bouclé yarn

The hat shown is made with S.R. Kertzer Super 10 Cotton: 100% mercerized cotton, 4.4 oz. (125 g)/ 250 yd. (228.6 m); Trendsetter Yarns Skye, 100% nylon, 1.75 oz. (50 g)/110 yd. (101 m); and Lion Brand Yarn Homespun: 98% acrylic, 2% polyester, 6 oz. (170 g)/185 yd. (169 m).

Yardage

40 yd. Super 10 Cotton #3553 Canary

4 yd. Super 10 Cotton #3454 Bubblegum

80 yd. Skye #1889 Carnation

30 yd. Homespun #790-389 Spring Green

Materials

16-in. U.S. size 4 circular needle

Four U.S. size 4 double-pointed needles

Stitch marker

Tapestry needle

Pom Pom maker ($1\frac{1}{2}$ in.)

GAUGE

22 sts = 4 in. with Super 10 Cotton

Directions

HAT BASE

With circ needles and Homespun, CO 80 sts. Place a st marker on right needle and, beginning Rnd 1, join CO sts together making sure that sts do not become twisted on needle.

Rnd 1: P.

Rnd 2: P.

Rnds 3–6: K.

Cut Homespun and attach Skye.

K1 rnd. Attach Canary.

BOBBLE ROUND 1

*MB (see p. 133 for Bobble instructions) with

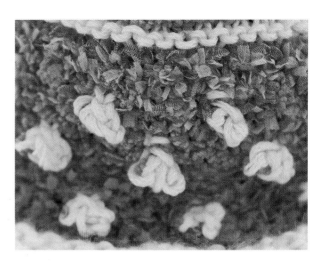

Canary. Drop Canary and K4 with Skye; rep from *
to end of rnd.

Drop Canary and K3 rnds with Skye.

BOBBLE ROUND 2

K2 with Skye. *MB with Canary. Drop Canary and
K4 with Skye; rep from *. End K3 with Skye.

Drop Canary and K3 rnds with Skye.

Rep Bobble Round 1.

Drop Canary and K3 rnds with Skye.

STRIPES

*Drop Skye and K1 rnd with Canary. P1 rnd. Drop
Canary and K3 rnds with Skye. Rep from *
4 times. After last rnd, cut Canary and attach
Homespun.

CROWN DECREASES

Dec Rnd 1: *K8, K2tog; rep from * to end of rnd.

Dec Rnd 2: *K7, K2tog; rep from * to end of rnd.

Continue in established pattern, changing to dpns
when necessary, until approx 4–6 sts rem. Cut
the yarn, leaving a 6-in. tail. Using a tapestry
needle, thread the tail through the rem sts on
the needles. Pull the yarn, gathering sts tightly
together, then secure the tail on the WS of
the work.

WELT

Thread a tapestry needle with Bubblegum, pinch
the hat together between the top of the second
Canary stripe and the bottom of the fourth Canary
stripe, and create a welt (see p. 135) by sewing
the pieces together with evenly spaced running
stitches. Secure ends on WS of hat.

POM POM

Using Skye and Canary, make Pom Pom (see
p. 135) and attach to top of hat.

FINISHING

Weave in all loose ends.

Peppermint Candy Cap

Giant Pom Poms and a swirly-ridged crown make this cap perfect for your own little peppermint sweetie.

Sizing

Newborn (14-in. circumference) to 2 years (16-in. circumference)

Figures for larger size are given below in parentheses. Where only one set of figures appears, the directions apply to both sizes.

Yarn

DK Weight smooth yarn
DK Weight eyelash yarn

The hat shown is made with S.R. Kertzer Super 10 Cotton: 100% mercerized cotton, 4.4 oz. (125 g)/250 yd. (228.6 m) and Stylecraft Icicle: 62% polyester, 38% metallized polyester, 1.75 oz. (50 g)/87 yd. (80 m).

Yardage

60 (70) yd. Super 10 Cotton #3443 Shell Pink
25 yd. Super 10 Cotton #3722 Celery
10 yd. Super 10 Cotton #3997 Scarlet
40 yd. Super 10 Cotton #3475 Geranium
Small amount of Icicle #1140 Crystal

Materials

16-in. U.S. size 4 circular needle
Four U.S. size 4 double-pointed needles
Stitch marker
Tapestry needle
Pom Pom maker ($1\frac{1}{2}$ in.)

GAUGE

22 sts = 4 in. with Super 10 Cotton

Directions

HAT BASE

With circ needles and Scarlet, CO 72 (80) sts. Place a st marker on right needle and, beginning Rnd 1, join CO sts together making sure that sts do not become twisted on needle.

Rnd 1: P.

Rnd 2: Cut Scarlet. K entire rnd with Shell Pink.

Rnd 3: P with Shell Pink.

INCREASE ROUND

With Shell Pink *K1, K1f&b; rep from * to end of
rnd—108 (120) sts.

K with Shell Pink for a total of 12 rnds.

Drop Shell Pink. Attach Celery. *K1 rnd. P1 rnd.
Drop Celery, pick up Shell Pink, and K4 rnds;
drop Shell Pink, pick up Celery, and rep from *
until you have a total of 4 Celery ridges.

SWIRL TOP

Cut Shell Pink and Celery. Attach Geranium
and start dec rnds, changing to dpns when
necessary.

Dec Rnd 1: *K7 (8), K2tog; rep from * to end
of rnd.

Dec Rnd 2: *K6 (7), K2tog; rep from * to end
of rnd. Continue in established pattern, knitting
1 less st between decs. When 4–6 sts rem,
cut the yarn, leaving a 6-in. tail. Thread a tapestry
needle and pass it through the remaining sts left
on the needle. Bring the tail to the WS of the work.

Rnd 4: Drop Shell Pink. Attach Geranium and
K entire rnd.

Rnd 5: P with Geranium.

Rep Rnds 2–5 until you have 4 ridges of Shell Pink
and 3 ridges of Geranium. Cut Geranium, attach
Scarlet, and K entire rnd. P next rnd. Cut Scarlet
and pick up Shell Pink.

FINISHING

Weave in all loose ends.

Thread a tapestry needle with Geranium, pinch the
hat at the first Celery pure rnd, and create a Welt
(see p. 135) by sewing together the top and
bottom pieces using even running stitches.

Using Shell Pink and Icicle, make three Pom Poms
(see p. 135) and attach them securely to the top
of the hat.

Firecracker Topper

What a great hat for the summertime! A traditional sailor shape with a sizzling, glittery topper will bring a little pizzazz to any Fourth of July celebration.

Sizing

Newborn (14-in. circumference) to 2 years (18-in. circumference)

Figures for larger size are given below in parentheses. Where only one set of figures appears, the directions apply to both sizes.

Yarn

DK Weight smooth yarn

DK Weight eyelash yarn

The hat shown is made with S.R. Kertzer Super 10 Cotton: 100% mercerized cotton, 4.4 oz. (125 g)/250 yd. (228.6 m) and Stylecraft Icicle: 62% polyester, 38% metallized polyester, 1.75 oz. (50 g)/87 yd. (80 m).

Yardage

40 (50) yd. Super 10 Cotton #3997 Scarlet

30 (40) yd. Super 10 Cotton White

30 (40) yd. Super 10 Cotton #3871 Royal

20 yd. Super 10 Cotton #3533 Daffodil

2 yd. Icicle #1141 Polar

Materials

16-in. U.S. size 4 circular needle

Four U.S. size 4 double-pointed needles

Two stitch markers

Tapestry needle

GAUGE

22 sts = 4 in. with Super 10 Cotton

SEED STITCH

Rnd 1: *K1, P1; rep from * to end of rnd.

All other rnds: K the P sts and P the K sts.

Directions

HAT BASE

Using circ needles and Scarlet, CO 82 (100) sts. Place a st marker on right needle and, beginning Rnd 1, join CO sts together making sure that sts do not become twisted on needle.

Note: Always keep unworked yarn on the WS of your work and sl sts pw.

Rnd 1: P.

Rnd 2: Drop Scarlet and attach White. With White
   *K1, sl 1 wyib; rep from * to end of rnd.

Rnd 3: With White *P1, sl 1 wyib; rep from * to
   end of rnd.

Rnd 4: Drop White. K with Scarlet for entire rnd.

Rnd 5: P with Scarlet.

Rep Rnds 2–5 twice.

Cut White, and with Scarlet work Seed st for
   $1^1/_2$ ($2^1/_2$) in. Cut Scarlet and attach Daffodil.
   K1 rnd. Bind off pw.

Holding the hat with the RS facing you, bend the
   Seed st work down to expose the WS of the hat
   base. You will see the White and Scarlet loops
   from the initial ribbing. With Royal pick up 82 (100)
   sts (the loops) evenly spaced around the hat. *K4
   rnds. Drop Royal and attach White. K4 rnds. Rep
   from * until you have 3 Royal stripes. Cut Royal and
   attach Scarlet. K1 rnd, P1 rnd, placing a second st
   marker halfway across work.

DECREASE ROUNDS

**Drop Scarlet and pick up White.

Dec Rnd: *K to 2 sts before marker, K2tog, sl marker,
   sl 1, K1, psso. Rep from * at second marker.

Rep Dec Rnd twice more, for a total of 3 Dec Rnds.

RIDGE ROUND

Drop White and pick up Scarlet. K1 rnd, P1 rnd.

Rep from **, dec at the markers on every White
   rnd and placing sts on dpns when necessary.
   Work until you have created 6 Scarlet ridges and
   you have approx 8 sts left on the needles. Cut
   the yarn, leaving a 6-in. tail. Using a tapestry
   needle, thread the tail through the remaining sts
   on the needles. Pull the yarn, gathering sts tightly
   together, then secure the tail on the WS of
   the hat.

FIRECRACKER TOPPER

Cut 10–15 Icicle strands (approx 6 in. long) and
   tie them together at the center using a strand of
   Icicle. Fold this bundle in half, making a tassel,
   and secure it to the tip of the hat by tying the tails
   to the WS of the hat.

FINISHING

Weave in all ends. Make five 2-in.-long I-Cords (see
   p. 134) with Daffodil. Using a tapestry needle,
   thread the I-Cord tail through to the same end as
   the CO tail. Use both tails to attach each I-Cord
   to the tip of the hat.

Fold the Scarlet Seed st "ruffle" down to the bottom
   of the hat to create a faux welt for the base of
   the hat.

Hearts & Flowers Hat

Silk flowers make a wonderful addition to this ruffled confection. Make it for your sweet valentine to wear all year 'round!

Sizing

6 to 14 months (16-in. circumference)

Yarn

DK Weight smooth yarn

The hat shown is made with S.R. Kertzer Super 10 Cotton: 100% mercerized cotton, 4.4 oz. (125 g)/250 yd. (228.6 m).

Yardage

5 yd. Super 10 Cotton #3443 Shell Pink

90 yd. Super 10 Cotton #3997 Scarlet

40 yd. Super 10 Cotton #3454 Bubblegum

Materials

16-in. U.S. size 4 circular needle

Four U.S. size 4 double-pointed needles

Stitch marker

Tapestry needle

Silk flower (found at any craft store)

Small piece of Velcro® (optional)

GAUGE

22 sts = 4 in.

Directions

HAT BASE

With circ needles and Scarlet, CO 140 sts. Place a st marker on right needle and, beginning Rnd 1, join CO sts together making sure that sts do not become twisted on needle.

Rnd 1: P.

Rnd 2: K.

Rnd 3: P.

Rnd 4: Drop Scarlet, attach Bubblegum, and K entire rnd.

Rnd 5: P.

Rep Rnds 4 and 5, alternating Scarlet and Bubblegum in Rnd 4, until you have 4 ridges of Bubblegum. Cut Bubblegum and pick up Scarlet. K1 rnd.

Next Rnd: Turn needles and work in opposite direction for the rest of the project. This ensures

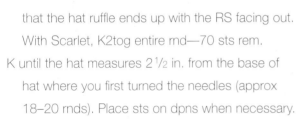

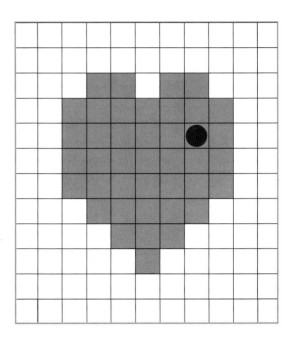

HEART CHART • Work Duplicate Stitch hearts all around the hat using Bubblegum except for one done in Shell Pink. And don't forget to mark the heart of each heart with a French Knot!

that the hat ruffle ends up with the RS facing out. With Scarlet, K2tog entire rnd—70 sts rem.

K until the hat measures 2 1/2 in. from the base of hat where you first turned the needles (approx 18–20 rnds). Place sts on dpns when necessary.

DECREASE ROUNDS

Dec Rnd 1: *K8, k2tog; rep from * for entire rnd. K5 rnds.

Dec Rnd 2: *K7, k2tog; rep from * for entire rnd. K5 rnds.

Dec Rnd 3: *K6, k2tog; rep from * for entire rnd. K3 rnds.

Dec Rnd 4: *K5, k2tog; rep from * for entire rnd. K2 rnds.

Dec Rnd 5: *K4, k2tog; rep from * for entire rnd. K2 rnds.

Dec Rnd 6: *K3, k2tog; rep from * for entire rnd. K1 rnd.

Dec Rnd 7: *K2, k2tog; rep from * for entire rnd.

Dec Rnd 8: *K1, k2tog; rep from * for entire rnd. K2tog until 4–6 sts rem.

Cut yarn, leaving a 6-in. tail. Using a tapestry needle, thread the tail through the remaining sts on the needles. Pull the yarn, gathering sts tightly together, then secure the tail on the WS of the hat.

FINISHING

Weave in all ends. Following the graph on the facing page and using Duplicate Stitch (see p. 133), decorate the hat with hearts using Bubblegum and Shell Pink. With Scarlet, create French Knots (see p. 134) in the "heart" of each heart.

Fold striped ruffle and secure to hat base at regular intervals with a tapestry needle and Scarlet. Attach a silk flower to the tip of the hat using Velcro for easy removal, or sew flower securely to tip of hat.

Humdingers

Black & Bright Beret

Vibrant colors set against black make this hat absolutely smashing. Fun "fingers" are a great finishing touch.

Sizing

6 months (14-in. circumference) to 2 years (16-in. circumference)

Figures for larger size are given below in parentheses. Where only one set of figures appears, the directions apply to both sizes.

Yarn

DK Weight smooth yarn

The hat shown is made with S.R. Kertzer Super 10 Cotton: 100% mercerized cotton, 4.4 oz. (125 g)/ 250 yd. (228.6 m) and S.R. Kertzer Super 10 Cotton Multi: 100% mercerized cotton, 3.5 oz. (100 g)/220 yd. (201 m).

Yardage

40 (50) yd. Super 10 Cotton Black
30 yd. Super 10 Cotton #3873 Lapis
40 yd. Super 10 Cotton #3062 Turquoise
30 yd. Super 10 Cotton Multi #2016 Carousel

Materials

16-in. U.S. size 4 circular needle
Four U.S. size 4 double-pointed needles
Four stitch markers
Tapestry needle

GAUGE

22 sts = 4 in.

SEED STITCH

Rnd 1: *K1, P1; rep from * to end of rnd.
All other rnds: K the P sts and P the K sts.

Directions

HAT BASE

With circ needle and Lapis, CO 72 (88) sts. Place a st marker on right needle and, beginning Rnd 1, join CO sts together making sure that sts do not become twisted on needle.

Note: Always keep unworked yarn on the WS of your work and sl sts pw.

Rnd 1: P. Drop Lapis and attach Turquoise.

Rnd 2: With Turquoise *K1, sl 1; rep from * to end of rnd.

Rnd 3: With Turquoise *P1, sl 1; rep from * to end of rnd.

Rnd 4: Drop Turquoise. K with Lapis.

Rnd 5: P with Lapis.

Rep Rnds 2–5 three times to create 3 Lapis ridges. Cut Lapis.

Next Rnd: K with Turquoise.

RUFFLE

Inc Rnd: With Turquoise, *K2, K1f&b; rep from * to end of rnd. Work Seed st for 1 1/2 (2) in. There should be 108 (132) sts on the needle.

Cut Turquoise. Attach Lapis and K1 rnd.

FINGERS

Attach Multi. *Using the Cable Cast-On (see p. 133) and Multi, CO 5 sts, then BO 5 sts. K3 sts with Lapis. Rep from * for remainder of rnd. Cut Multi and K1 rnd with Lapis. BO all sts pw.

Holding the hat with the RS facing you, bend the Turquoise ruffle down and expose the hat base. With Black, pick up 72 (88) sts (Lapis loops) evenly spaced around the hat. K for approx 3 in.

CROWN RIDGE

Cut Black and attach Lapis. K1 rnd, P1 rnd.

Drop Lapis and attach Turquoise. K1 rnd.

Cut Turquoise and pick up Lapis. K1 rnd, P1 rnd.

MULTI CROWN

Cut all yarn and attach Multi. K1 rnd and divide work into 4 equal parts, placing a st marker after every 18 (22) sts.

SWIRL TOP DECREASES

On every rnd, at every st marker, make the following dec (putting sts on dpns when necessary): Sl marker, sl 1, K1, psso. Continue until 4 sts rem. Cut Multi and attach Turquoise.

TOP STEM

Place rem 4 sts onto a dpn. With Turquoise, work I-Cord (see p. 134) for 2 in. Cut all yarn, leaving a 6-in. tail. Thread tail through a tapestry needle

and pass it through the remaining sts on dpn needle. Carefully pass needle and tails through the center of the I-Cord into the WS of the crown and secure.

FINISHING

Weave in all loose ends. Push the Turquoise ruffle down to bottom of hat and let the fingers stand up straight and tall.

Circles & Dots Beret

Chic baby couture is so easy to create. Simply add circles and red dots with a running stitch and French Knots. Très belle!

Sizing

6 months (14-in. circumference) to 2 years (16- or 18-in. circumference)

Figures for larger sizes are given below in parentheses. Where only one set of figures appears, the directions apply to all sizes.

Yarn

DK Weight smooth yarn

The hat shown is made with S.R. Kertzer Super 10 Cotton: 100% mercerized cotton, 4.4 oz. (125 g)/250 yd. (228.6 m).

Yardage

80 (100, 100) yd. Super 10 Cotton #3873 Lapis

10 yd. Super 10 Cotton #3997 Scarlet

25 yd. Super 10 Cotton #3533 Daffodil

Materials

16-in. U.S. size 4 circular needle

Four U.S. size 4 double-pointed needles

Stitch marker

Tapestry needle

GAUGE

22 sts = 4 in.

Directions

HAT BASE

CO 70 (90, 110) sts with circ needle and Lapis. Place a st marker on right needle and, beginning Rnd 1, join CO sts together making sure that sts do not become twisted on needle.

Rnd 1: P.

Next Rnds: K7 (10, 15) rnds.

INCREASE ROUNDS

Inc Rnd 1: *K4, K1f&b; rep from * to end of rnd. You should have 84 (108, 132) sts. K2 rnds.

Inc Rnd 2: *K5, K1f&b; rep from * to end of rnd. You should have 98 (126, 154) sts. K2 rnds.

Inc Rnd 3: *K6, K1f&b; rep from * to end of rnd. You should have 112 (144,176) sts. K2 rnds.

Now you've completed a total of 17 (20, 25) rnds.

Dec Rnd 2: *K7 (5, 5), K2tog; rep from * to end of rnd. K2 (4, 5) rnds.

Continue in established pattern, knitting one less st between decs and putting sts on dpns when necessary, until you have completed K1, K2tog, and approx 6 sts rem. Cut the yarn, leaving a 6-in. tail. Thread a tapestry needle and pass it through the remaining sts on the needle. Bring tail to the WS of the work and secure.

RIDGE ROWS

Drop Lapis and attach Daffodil.

Rnd 1: K.

Rnd 2: P.

Cut Daffodil. Pick up Lapis and K1 rnd.

FINISHING

Weave in all loose ends. Thread a tapestry needle with Daffodil and, using a running stitch, decorate the brim of the hat with circles.

Here's a tip: Use a quarter as a guide to make sure the circles are evenly spaced and roughly the same size.

TOP DECREASES

Dec Rnd 1: *K8 (6, 6), K2tog; repeat from * to end of rnd. K2 (4, 5) rnds.

Continuing with Daffodil, embroider a concentric circle on the top of the hat. Thread a tapestry needle with Scarlet and create French Knots (see p. 134) in the centers of the circles on the brim as well as the one in the center of the hat. Voila!

Heavenly Harlequin Hat

This hat is a little zany and a whole lot of fun. French Knots and squiggles on top guarantee that it will stand out in a crowd!

Sizing

Newborn (12-in. circumference) to 2 years (14- or 16-in. circumference)

Figures for larger sizes are given below in parentheses. Where only one set of figures appears, the directions apply to all sizes.

Yarn

DK Weight smooth yarn

The hat shown is made with S.R. Kertzer Super 10 Cotton: 100% mercerized cotton, 4.4 oz. (125 g)/250 yd (228.6 m).

Yardage

40 (50, 60) yd. Super 10 Cotton #3936 Wisteria

40 (50, 50) yd. Super 10 Cotton #3535 Key Lime

30 yd. Super 10 Cotton #3042 Nectarine

10 (20, 20) yd. Super 10 Cotton #3533 Daffodil

Materials

16-in. U.S. size 4 circular needle

Four U.S. size 4 straight needles

Stitch marker

Tapestry needle

GAUGE

22 sts = 4 in.

Directions

HAT BASE

With circ needles and Key Lime, CO 70 (80, 90) sts. Place a st marker on right needle and, beginning Rnd 1, join CO sts together making sure that sts do not become twisted on needle.

Rnd 1: P.

Rnd 2: *Attach Daffodil and MB (see p. 133 for Bobble instructions). Drop Daffodil, pick up Key Lime, K4; rep from * to end of rnd.

Rnd 3: K with Key Lime.

Rnd 4: Drop Key Lime, pick up Daffodil. K entire rnd.

Rnd 5: P with Daffodil. Drop Daffodil, pick up Key Lime.

Next 4 (5, 6) rnds: K with Key Lime.

Next Rnd: Drop Key Lime, pick up Daffodil. K entire rnd.

Next Rnd: P with Daffodil.

Cut Daffodil and Key Lime. Attach Wisteria. K4 (6, 8) rnds.

DECREASE ROUNDS

Dec Rnd 1: *K8, K2tog; rep from * to end of rnd. K4 rnds.

Dec Rnd. 2: *K7, K2tog; rep from * to end of rnd. K4 rnds.

Continue in established pattern, knitting one less st between decs and changing to dpns when necessary until you have completed K3, K2tog. K2 rnds.

Next Dec Rnd: *K2, K2tog; rep from * to end of rnd. K2 rnds.

Next Dec Rnd: *K1, K2tog; rep from * to end of rnd.

Next Dec Rnd: K2tog for the entire rnd.

Cut yarn, leaving a 6-in. tail, and thread a tapestry needle. Pass the tapestry needle through the remaining sts. Bring to WS of work and secure.

I-CORD

With Nectarine and 2 dpns, CO 3 sts. Make an I-Cord (see p. 134) approx 36 in. long. Thread a tapestry needle and pass it through the sts on the needle to BO. Cut the yarn, leaving a long tail to sew the I-Cord onto the hat. Decorate the hat with the I-Cord in a spiral pattern (at right).

SQUIGGLE TOPPERS

Make 3 Daffodil and 2 Key Lime I-Cords. Using 2 dpns, CO 2 sts and work until I-Cords are approximately 8 in. long. Cut yarn, leaving 4-in. tails. Thread each tail through a tapestry needle and slip through the sts on the needle to BO. Pass the needle through the I-Cords. Bring both tails through the peak of the hat, pulling tight to make each I-Cord scrunch up into a little squiggle.

FINISHING

Weave in all loose ends. Thread a tapestry needle with Wisteria and, using Duplicate Stitch (see p. 133), make diagonal sts on the second Key Lime band. For the final touch, use Nectarine to make small French Knots (see p. 134) between the Daffodil bobbles on the bottom Key Lime band. Ta-da! Heavenly Harlequin Hat!

Wee Wild One

A big smile lies under that big sparkling nose. Add some wild hair and a pair of glittery ears, and you have a friendly face for your little wild one.

Sizing

6 months to 2 years (16-in. circumference)

Yarn

DK Weight smooth yarn

The hat shown is made with S.R. Kertzer Super 10 Cotton: 100% mercerized cotton, 4.4 oz. (125 g)/ 250 yd. (228.6 m) and Stylecraft Icicle: 62% polyester, 38% metallized polyester, 1.75 oz. (50 g)/87 yd. (80 m).

Yardage

60 yd. Super 10 Cotton #3446 Cotton Candy or #3841 Caribbean

15 yd. Super 10 Cotton #3936 Wisteria

15 yd. Super 10 Cotton #3722 Celery

2 yd. Super 10 Cotton #3454 Bubblegum

1 yd. Super 10 Cotton Black

20 yd. Icicle #1143 Artic (blue) or #1140 Crystal (pink)

Materials

16-in. U.S. size 4 circular needle

One pair U.S. size 4 straight needles

Stitch marker

Tapestry needle

Pom Pom maker (1 in.)

GAUGE

22 sts = 4 in. with Super 10 Cotton

Directions

HAT BASE

With circ needle and Cotton Candy/Caribbean, CO 70. Place a st marker on right needle and, beginning Rnd 1, join CO sts together making sure that sts do not become twisted on needle.

Rnd 1: P.

Rnds 2–25: K.

Row 1 (RS): K35.

Row 2: P.

Row 3: K1, sl 1, K1, psso. Work until 3 sts rem, K2tog, K1.

Rep Rows 2 and 3 until 23 sts remain. P1 row. Cut Cotton Candy/Caribbean and attach Icicle. K every row (Garter st) for the remainder of the ear, continuing decs as established until 4–5 sts rem on the needle. Cut the yarn, leaving a 6-in. tail. Thread the tapestry needle and pass it through the rem sts. Secure to WS of work.

Attach Cotton Candy/Caribbean where the work was divided for the first ear and create the second ear following the same directions.

FINISHING

With Cotton Candy/Caribbean, thread the tapestry needle with tails and sew the Wild One's head closed. Weave in all loose ends.

SPARKLY NOSE

Using Cotton Candy/Caribbean and matching Icicle, make a large Pom Pom (see p. 135) and attach it to the front of hat below the seam and hair.

Embroider eyes and a big grin onto the face of the hat using Black and Bubblegum. See the photograph on the facing page for visual reference.

HAIR

Attach Celery and Wisteria. *MB (see p. 133 for Bobble instructions) with Wisteria. K1 with Cotton Candy/Caribbean. Using the Cable Cast-On (see p. 133), pick up Celery and create one "hair" as follows: CO 8 sts. BO those 8 sts. K1 with Cotton Candy/Caribbean; rep from * for entire rnd. Now our wee one has some wild hair!

EARS

For the ears, divide the work in half and work back and forth on straight needles—not in the round—for the remainder of the hat.

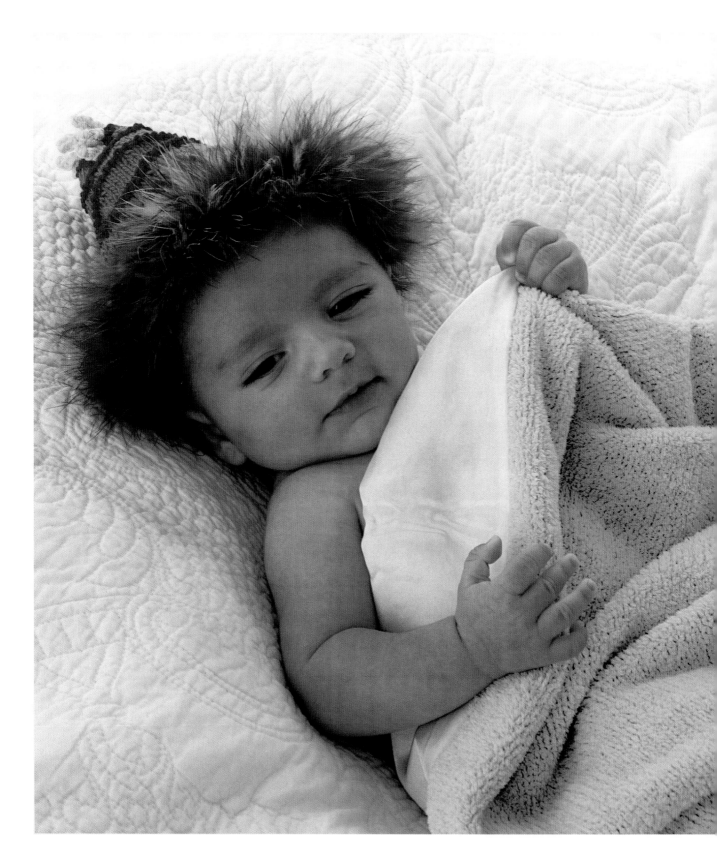

Feathers & Fringe Fedora

My favorite color combinations make this an eye-popping topper. Boas are easy to find in any craft store and make a fabulous fringe for this unique hat.

Sizing

Newborn (14-in. circumference) to 2 years (18-in. circumference)

Figures for larger size are given below in parentheses. Where only one set of figures appears, the directions apply to both sizes.

Yarn

DK Weight smooth yarn

The hat shown is made with S.R. Kertzer Super 10 Cotton: 100% mercerized cotton, 4.4 oz. (125 g)/ 250 yd. (228.6 m).

Yardage

30 (35) yd. Super 10 Cotton #3997 Scarlet

25 yd. Super 10 Cotton #3533 Daffodil

30 (40) yd. Super 10 Cotton #3764 Peppermint

40 (50) yd. Super 10 Cotton # 3402 Nectarine

1 yd. multicolored feather boa (found in any craft supply store)

Materials

16-in. U.S. size 4 circular needle

Four U.S. size 4 double-pointed needles

Stitch marker

Tapestry needle

GAUGE

22 sts = 4 in.

Directions

HAT BASE

With circ needle and Peppermint, CO 72 (100) sts. Place a st marker on right needle and, beginning Rnd 1, join CO sts together making sure that sts do not become twisted on needle.

Rnd 1: P.

Rnd 2: K.

Rnd 3: P.

Rnds 4–11: K.

Rep Rnds 1–3. Cut Peppermint and attach
Nectarine.

RIDGE PATTERN

**With Nectarine K6 (10) rnds. Drop Nectarine.

Dec Rnd: Attach Scarlet and *K7 (8), K2tog; rep
from * for entire rnd.

Next Rnd: P with Scarlet.

Drop Scarlet. Pick up Nectarine and rep from **.
Continue with established Ridge Pattern for
a total of 6 Scarlet Ridges, knitting 1 less st
between decs and putting sts on dpns when
necessary.

FRINGE

Cut Scarlet and attach Daffodil. *Using the Cable
Cast-On (see p. 133), CO 5 sts, then BO those
5 sts. K1 st. Rep from * for the entire rnd. K1
rnd. Cut the yarn, leaving a 6-in. tail. Thread a
tapestry needle and pass it through the remaining
sts. Pull the yarn tight to gather the fringe and
secure it to the WS of the work.

FINISHING

With Daffodil, and using the bottom photograph at
right as a reference, create French Knots (see
p. 134) on the first band of Nectarine. Attach the
boa to the base of the hat along the Peppermint
band with fabric glue or by sewing it on with a
tapestry needle and yarn.

Bull's-Eye Beret

Ooh la la! The chenille yarn makes this beret so soft and warm. With an extra-large Pom Pom smack in the middle of the red bull's-eye, this beret is so very chic!

Sizing

6 months (14-in. circumference) to 18 months (18-in. circumference)

Figures for larger size are given below in parentheses. Where only one set of figures appears, the directions apply to both sizes.

Yarn

DK Weight smooth yarn

Bulky Weight chenille yarn

The hat shown is made with S.R. Kertzer Super 10 Cotton: 100% mercerized cotton, 4.4 oz. (125 g)/250 yd. (228.6 m) and Lion Brand Yarn Chenille Thick & Quick: 91% acrylic, 9% rayon, 100 yd. (91 m).

Yardage

40 (50) yd. Super 10 Cotton #3873 Lapis

20 (30) yd. Super 10 Cotton Black

10 yd. Super 10 Cotton #3997 Scarlet

20 yd. Chenille Thick & Quick #950-131 Forest Green

Materials

16-in. U.S. size 4 circular needle

16-in. U.S. size 9 circular needle

Four U.S. size 4 double-pointed needles

Stitch marker

Tapestry needle

Pom Pom maker

GAUGE

22 sts = 4 in. with Super 10 Cotton and size 4 needle

Directions

HAT BASE

With circ needle and Lapis, CO 72 (90) sts. Place a st marker on right needle and, beginning Rnd 1, join CO sts together making sure that sts do not become twisted on needle.

Rnd 1: P.

Next 7 (10) Rnds: K.

Cut Lapis. Attach Chenille and K1 rnd with size

Drop Lapis and pick up Black. K4 (6) rnds.

Drop Black and pick up Lapis. K5 rnds.

Cut Lapis and pick up Black. K1 rnd. Cut Black and attach Scarlet.

DECREASE ROUNDS

Dec Rnd 1: *K7 (8), K2tog; rep from * to end of rnd.

Dec Rnd 2: *K6 (7), K2tog; rep from * to end of rnd.

Continue in established pattern, knitting 1 less st between decs until 4–6 sts rem, putting sts on dpns when necessary.

Cut the yarn, leaving a 6-in. tail. Using a tapestry needle, thread the tail through the remaining sts on the needles. Pull the yarn, gathering sts tightly together, then secure the tail on the WS of the beret.

FINISHING

Weave in all loose ends. With Chenille, create a large Pom Pom (see p. 135) and attach it to the top of the beret.

9 circ needle. P1 rnd. Rep these 2 rnds for 8 (10) rnds. Cut Chenille. Attach Lapis and K6 (9) rnds with size 4 circ needle.

Drop Lapis and attach Black. K4 (6) rnds.

Drop Black and pick up Lapis. K5 (7) rnds.

Bobble Beanie

Colors swirl all around this bright beanie. The big bobbles and red crown are quick and easy to complete. A multicolored Pom Pom tops it off.

Sizing

6 months (14-in. circumference) to 2 years (16- or 18-in. circumference)

Figures for larger sizes are given below in parentheses. Where only one set of figures appears, the directions apply to all sizes.

Yarn

DK Weight smooth yarn

The hat shown is made with S.R. Kertzer Super 10 Cotton: 100% mercerized cotton, 4.4 oz. (125 g)/250 yd. (228.6 m) and S.R. Kertzer Super 10 Cotton Multi: 100% mercerized cotton, 3.5 oz. (100 g)/220 yd. (201 m).

Yardage

20 yd. Super 10 Cotton Black

40 (50, 55) yd. Super 10 Cotton #3997 Scarlet

30 yd. Super 10 Cotton #3533 Daffodil

5 yd. Super 10 Cotton #3764 Peppermint

5 yd. Super 10 Cotton #3873 Lapis

30 yd. Super 10 Cotton Multi #2016 Carousel

Materials

16-in. U.S. size 4 circular needle

Four U.S. size 4 double-pointed needles

Four stitch markers

Pom Pom maker (1½ in.)

GAUGE

22 sts = 4 in.

Directions

HAT BASE

With circ needle and Black, CO 72 (80, 96) sts.
Place a st marker on right needle and, beginning Rnd 1, join CO sts together making sure that sts do not become twisted on needle.

Rnds 1 & 3: P.

Rnd 2: K.

Rnd 4: Cut Black and attach Scarlet. K.

FIRST BOBBLE ROUND

Attach Multi. *MB (see p.133 for Bobble instructions), with Scarlet K7; rep from * to end of rnd. Drop Multi, and with Scarlet K5 rnds.

SECOND BOBBLE ROUND

With Scarlet K4. With Multi *MB, K7; rep from * to last 3 sts, K3.

Cut Scarlet and Multi and attach Black. K1 rnd, P1 rnd, K1 rnd.

Cut Black and attach Daffodil. K1 rnd, dividing work into 4 equal parts, and placing a st marker after every 18 (20, 24) sts.

INCREASE ROUNDS

K to 1 st before marker, K1f&b, sl marker, K1, K1f&b into next st. Continue working incs at each marker for 8 rnds—136 (144, 160) sts.

RIDGE ROUNDS

Cut Daffodil and attach Peppermint. K1 rnd. P1 rnd. Drop Peppermint and attach Lapis. K1 rnd. P1 rnd. Cut Lapis and pick up Peppermint. K1 rnd. P1 rnd. Cut Peppermint and attach Scarlet. K1 rnd.

SWIRL CROWN DECREASES

Dec Rnd 1: *K6, K2tog; rep from * to end of rnd.
Dec Rnd 2: *K5, K2tog; rep from * to end of rnd.

Continue in established pattern, knitting 1 less st between decs until you have completed K2, K2tog.

K5 (7, 9) rnds with no decreases. Cut yarn, leaving a 6-in. tail. Thread a tapestry needle and slip the tail through sts on needle and pull tightly.

FINISHING

Weave in all loose ends. Using all the bright colors in the hat, make a very full Pom Pom (see p. 135) and attach to peak of hat.

Squiggle Circus Beanie

Perfect for your little clown! Bright red squiggles are easy to make, and a green Pom Pom tops off this wonderfully silly hat.

Sizing

3 months (15-in. circumference) to 2 years (20-in. circumference)

Figures for larger size are given below in parentheses. Where only one set of figures appears, these directions apply to both sizes.

Yarn

DK Weight smooth yarn

The hat shown is made with S.R. Kertzer Super 10 Cotton: 100% mercerized cotton, 4.4 oz. (125g)/250 yd. (228.6 m).

Yardage

70 (80) yd. Super 10 Cotton #3997 Scarlet
40 (50) yd. Super 10 Cotton #3871 Royal
25 yd. Super 10 Cotton #3764 Peppermint
30 yd. Super 10 Cotton #3533 Daffodil

Materials

16-in. U.S. size 4 circular needle
Four U.S. size 4 double-pointed needles
Stitch marker
Tapestry needle
Pom Pom maker (1½ in.)

GAUGE
22 sts = 4 in.

Directions

HAT BASE

With circ needles and Royal, CO 80 (100) sts. Place a st marker on right needle and, beginning Rnd 1, join CO sts together making sure that sts do not become twisted on needle.

Rnd 1: P.

Rnd 2: K.

Rep these 2 rnds 3 times.

Attach Peppermint. *MB (see p. 133 for Bobble instructions) with Peppermint. K8 (9) with Royal; rep from * to end of rnd. Cut Peppermint.

between the bottom of the squiggles and the top of the Royal ridges. With Daffodil, pick up and K1 st in each "upward" loop at this join 80 (100) sts. K10 (14) rnds.

Cut Daffodil. Attach Royal and K1 rnd. P1 rnd.

Cut Royal. Attach Scarlet and K10 (15) rnds.

SWIRL CROWN

Dec Rnd 1: *K8, K2tog; rep from * to end of rnd.

Dec Rnd 2: *K7, K2tog; rep from * to end of rnd.

Continue in established pattern, knitting 1 less st between decs and putting sts on dpns when necessary, until you have approx 4–6 sts on the needle. Cut Scarlet and attach Royal.

With rem sts, work I-Cord (see p. 134) for approx 6 in. or desired length. Cut yarn, leaving a 6-in. tail. Using a tapestry needle, thread the tail through the remaining sts on the needle, then down into the center of the I-Cord, securing it to the WS of the beanie.

Using Royal, rep Rnds 1–2 three times.

Cut Royal. Attach Scarlet. K1 rnd.

Next Rnd: K1f&b into each st—160 (200) sts.

SQUIGGLES ROUND

Using the Cable Cast-On (see p. 133) and Scarlet, *CO 8 sts. BO those 8 sts. K4 (5). Rep from * for the entire rnd. Cut Scarlet.

Holding the hat with the WS in, bend the section of squiggles toward you and expose the join

FINISHING

Weave in all loose ends. With Peppermint, make a Pom Pom (see p. 135) and attach to the tip of the I-Cord.

Using Duplicate Stitch (see p. 133) and Scarlet, decorate the Daffodil section with 7 (8)-st circles, leaving 1 (2) sts between each circle. Refer to the photograph on the facing page for placement. Make French Knots (see p. 134) in the center of each circle with Peppermint.

Lemon Drop Crown

This shimmering yellow beret is as warm and bright as the sun! The sparkling details make it right for any special shindig.

Sizing

3 to 18 months (14-in. circumference)

Yarn

DK Weight smooth yarn

DK Weight eyelash yarn

The hat shown is made with S.R. Kertzer Super 10 Cotton: 100% mercerized cotton, 4.4 oz. (125 g)/ 250 yd. (228.6 m) and Stylecraft Icicle: 62% polyester, 38% metallized polyester, 1.75 oz. (50 g)/87 yd. (80 m).

Yardage

70 yd. Super 10 Cotton #3533 Daffodil

40 yd. Super 10 Cotton #3532 Soft Yellow

20 yd. Icicle #1142 Sunlight

Small amount of Super 10 Cotton #3454 Bubblegum

Materials

16-in. U.S. size 4 circular needle

Four U.S. size 4 double-pointed needles

Four stitch markers

Tapestry needle

Pom Pom maker (3 in.)

GAUGE

22 sts = 4 in. with Super 10 Cotton

Directions

HAT BASE

With circ needle and Daffodil, CO 72 sts. Place a st marker on right needle and, beginning Rnd 1, join CO sts together making sure sts do not become twisted on needle.

Note: Always keep unworked yarn on the WS of your work and sl sts pw.

Rnd 1: P.

Rnd 2: Drop Daffodil and attach Soft Yellow. With Soft Yellow *K1, sl 1 wyib; rep from * to end of rnd.

Rnd 3: With Soft Yellow *P1, sl 1 wyib; rep from * to end of rnd.

Rnd 4: Drop Soft Yellow. K with Daffodil for the entire rnd.

Rnd 5: P with Daffodil.

Rnds 6–13: Rep Rnds 2–5.

Cut Daffodil and with Soft Yellow K1 rnd, placing a st marker after every 18th st to divide work into 4 equal parts.

Make the following inc at each marker: Work to 1 st before marker and K1f&b into next st, sl marker, K1, K1f&b into next st. Continue making inc at each marker until you have K8 rnds. You should have 136 sts.

Cut Soft Yellow and attach Icicle. K1 rnd. P1 rnd.

Cut Icicle and attach Daffodil. K8 rnds, keeping the markers on the needle.

CROWN DECREASES

Dec Rnd 1: *K up to 2 sts before each marker, sl 1, K1, psso, sl marker, K1, K2tog; rep from * to end of rnd. Continue in established pattern, changing to the dpns when necessary.

When 4–7 sts rem, cut the yarn, leaving a 6-in. tail. Using a tapestry needle, thread the tail through the remaining sts on the needles. Pull the yarn, gathering sts tightly together, then secure the tail on the WS of the crown.

FINISHING

With Daffodil and Icicle, make a Pom Pom (see p. 135). Attach it to the top of the crown. Using

Icicle, place French Knots (see p. 134) along the Soft Yellow row, 3 on each side of the hat (see the photo on the facing page). With Icicle, make 1 French Knot on each quarter of the crown directly below the Pom Pom. With Bubblegum, place small French Knots below each Icicle French Knot (see the photo above).

Swirls & Cherries Beret

This sweet beret is perfect for little girls, and is oh-so-quick to create! Decorate the hat with swirls using an easy running stitch. The cherries are the finishers that complete this delightful hat.

Sizing

6 months to 2 years (16-in. circumference)

Yarn

DK Weight smooth yarn

The hat shown is made with S.R. Kertzer Super 10 Cotton: 100% mercerized cotton, 4.4 oz. (125 g)/250 yd. (228.6 m).

Yardage

60 yd. Super 10 Cotton #3443 Shell Pink

14 yd. Super 10 Cotton #3454 Bubblegum

30 yd. Super 10 Cotton #3997 Scarlet

3 yd. Super 10 Cotton #3722 Celery

Materials

16-in. U.S. size 4 circular needle

Four U.S. size 4 double-pointed needles

One pair U.S. size 4 straight needles

Four stitch markers

Tapestry needle

GAUGE

22 sts = 4 in.

Directions

HAT BASE

With circ needles and Scarlet, CO 80. Place a st marker on right needle and, beginning Rnd 1, join CO sts together making sure that sts do not become twisted on needle.

Rnd 1: P. Cut Scarlet and attach Shell Pink.

STRIPE PATTERN

Stripe 1: Using Shell Pink, K1 rnd, P1 rnd.

Stripe 2: Drop Shell Pink and attach Bubblegum. K1 rnd, P1 rnd.

Rep Stripes 1 and 2 for a total of 7 stripes, ending with a Shell Pink stripe.

Last Stripe: Attach Scarlet and K1 rnd, P1 rnd.

Cut Bubblegum and Scarlet. K1 rnd with Shell Pink, dividing the work into 4 equal parts by placing a st marker after every 20th stitch.

INCREASE ROUNDS

Next Rnd: K to 1 st before marker, K1f&b, sl
marker, K1, K1f&b into the next stitch. Continue
working incs at each marker for 8 rnds. You
should have 144 sts.

RIDGE ROUNDS

Drop Shell Pink and attach Celery. K1 rnd, P1 rnd.
Cut Celery. K1 rnd with Shell Pink.

CROWN DECREASES

Dec Rnds: On each rnd and at every marker,
make the following decs: Work to 2 sts before
a marker, sl 1, K1, psso, sl marker, K1, K2tog.
Continue in established pattern, placing sts on dpns
when necessary. When approx 5–7 sts rem, drop
Shell Pink and attach Celery. Work I-Cord (see
p. 134) for 12 rows. Cut all yarn, leaving a 6-in.
tail. Thread a tapestry needle and pass it through
the remaining sts. Carefully pass the needle
and tails through the center of the I-Cord into
the WS of the crown and secure. Weave in all
loose ends.

CHERRIES

With Scarlet and straight needles, CO 1 st. K1f&b
twice, K1, into that st, creating 5 sts from 1.
K5 rows (Garter st).

Dec Rows: Sl 1, K1, psso, K1, K2tog. Cut the
yarn, leaving a 4-in. tail. Thread a tapestry needle

and pass it through the sts. Tie the CO and BO
tails together to form a ball. Make three cherries.
Attach each cherry to the tip of the Celery I-Cord by
threading a tapestry needle and bringing the tail
through the center of the I-Cord to the WS of the
crown. Tie each cherry securely and scrunch
the I-Cord a bit so that it looks like a stem.

RUNNING STITCH SWIRLS

Thread a tapestry needle with Scarlet. Using
the photograph on the facing page as a
reference, embroider as many swirls on the
band as you like.

Abbreviations

approx	approximately
beg	beginning
BO	bind off
circ	circular
CO	cast on
cont	continue
dec	decrease/decreases/decreasing
dpn(s)	double-pointed needle(s)
inc	increase/increases/increasing
K	knit
K1f&b	knit in the front and in the back of the same stitch
K2tog	knit 2 stitches together
kw	knitwise
M1	make 1 stitch
MB	make bobble
P	Purl
psso	pass slipped stitch over
pw	purlwise
rem	remaining
rep	repeat
rnd	round
RS	right side
skp	slip 1, knit 1, pass slipped stitch over knit 1
sl 1	slip 1 stitch
st(s)	stitch(es)
St st	stockinette stitch
tog	together
WS	wrong side
wyib	with yarn in back of work
yd	yard/yards
YO	yarn over

Special Stitches

Here are the stitches I use to give my hats a little something extra special. Read through the instructions and step-by-step illustrations before you start knitting and you'll have no problem with any of the fun touches that make each hat unique.

Bobble

With desired color yarn, K1, P1, K1 in the next st to make 3 sts from 1. Turn and K3. Turn and K3, then lift the second and third sts over the first st on the right needle.

Cable Cast-On

Insert right needle between first 2 sts on left needle. Wrap yarn as if to knit. Draw yarn through to complete st and slip this new st onto left needle.

Duplicate Stitch

Thread a tapestry needle with the desired color yarn. Bring the needle through from the WS of the work to the base of the knit st you wish to cover with a duplicate st on the front side. Insert the needle directly under the base of the knit st that lies above the st you wish to cover. Bring the needle down and insert it at the base of the same knit st. Bring the tip of the needle out at the base of the next st you wish to cover and repeat this process until you have covered all the desired sts in the design.

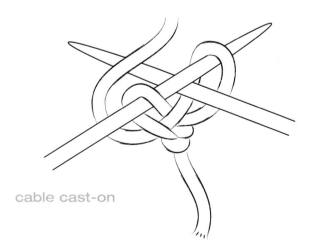

cable cast-on

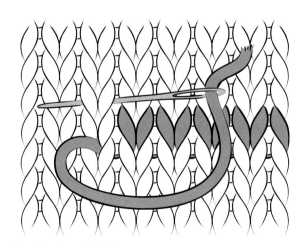

duplicate stitch

French Knot

Thread a tapestry needle with yarn and bring it from the WS of the work to the RS at the point where you wish to place the French Knot. Holding the yarn down with your left thumb, wind the yarn 3 times (for a small knot) or 4 to 6 times (for a large knot) around the needle. Still holding the yarn firmly, twist the needle back to the starting point and insert it close to where the yarn first emerged. Still holding the yarn down with your left thumb, slowly pull the yarn through to the WS to create a French Knot. Secure each knot on WS.

french knot

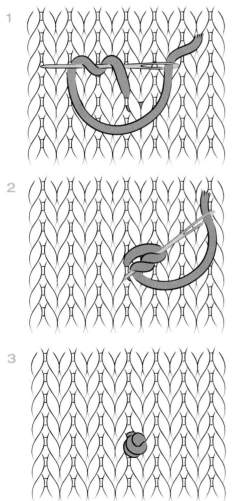

1

2

3

I-Cord

With two dpns, work I-Cord as follows: K4 to 6 sts. *Do not turn work. Slide sts to other end of needle, pull the yarn around the back, and knit the sts as usual. Repeat from * for desired length of cord.

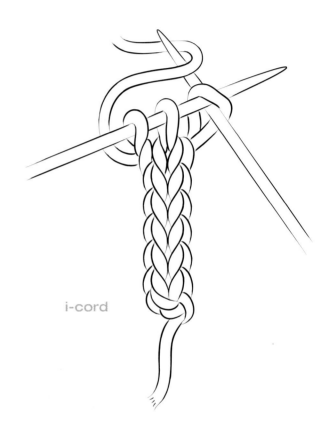

i-cord

M1 Increase

With the left needle tip, lift the strand between the last st you have knitted and the next st on your left needle. Knit into the back of that st. One st has been made.

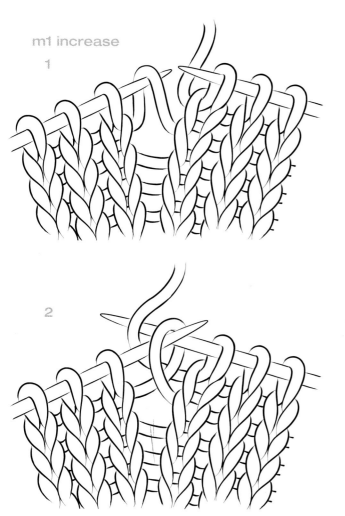

m1 increase
1

2

Pom Pom

Many knitting books give directions that require the knitter to make a Pom Pom maker, usually by cutting out a cardboard circle, figuring out the dimensions, and going from there. I have found that investing in an inexpensive Pom Pom maker (the cost is usually under $4.00) is the way to go. The one I like best is plastic and comes in several sizes, so I can make Pom Poms that are very small or extra-large. For all the Pom Poms in this book, I used a maker that had a $1^1/2$-in. to $2^1/2$-in. diameter. Always remember that the trick for a good, full Pom Pom is to wrap the yarn around the maker as many times as possible. Your Pom Pom will be full and stand proud!

Welt

Create a small welt by passing the needle over and under the pieces of knitting that you have "pinched" together, for example, at the side and crown of the hat. Weave both pieces (the side and crown) together using evenly spaced running sts that are approx $1/4$ in. from the crown edge. Sewing the two pieces together in this way will create a slight thickening or "welt" along the edge of the crown.

Standard Yarn Weights

NUMBERED BALL	DESCRIPTION	STS/4 IN.	NEEDLE SIZE
1 SUPER FINE	Sock, baby, fingering	27–32	2.25–3.25 mm (U.S. 1–3)
2 FINE	Sport, baby	23–26	3.25–3.75 mm (U.S. 3–5)
3 LIGHT	DK, light worsted	21–24	3.75–4.5 mm (U.S. 5–7)
4 MEDIUM	Worsted, afghan, Aran	16–20	4.5–5.5 mm (U.S. 7–9)
5 BULKY	Chunky, craft, rug	12–15	5.5–8.0 mm (U.S. 9–11)
6 SUPER BULKY	Bulky, roving	6–11	8 mm and larger (U.S. 11 and larger)

Sources

DEBBY WARE KNITWARES
PO Box 53
Rapidan, VA 22733
www.debbyware.com

LION BRAND YARN
34 West 15t Street
New York, NY 10011
www.lionbrand.com

S.R. KERTZER
6060 Burnside Court
Mississauga, ON
Canada L5T 2T5
www.kertzer.com

TRENDSETTER YARNS
16745 Saticoy Street
Van Nuys, CA 91406
www.trendsetteryarns.com